Tipbook Vocals

The Singing Voice

The Complete Guide

Hugo Pinksterboer

Tipbook Vocals The Singing Voice

The Complete Guide

The Complete Guide to Your Instrument!

First edition published in 2002 by
The Tipbook Company bv, The Netherlands
Fifth edition published in 2008 by
Hal Leonard Books
An Imprint of Hal Leonard Corporation
7777 West Bluemound Road
Milwaukee, WI 53213

Trade Book Division Editorial Offices
19 West 21st Street, New York, NY 10010

Printed in The United States of America

Book design by Gijs Bierenbroodspot

Library of Congress Cataloging-in-Publication Data
Pinksterboer, Hugo.
Tipbook vocals : the complete guide /
by Hugo Pinksterboer. — 5th ed.
p. cm.
Includes bibliographical references and index.
ISBN 978-1-4234-5622-3 (pbk.)
1. Singing—Instruction and study. I. Title.
MT893.P46 2008
783—dc22

2008040099

www.halleonard.com

Thanks!

For their information, their expertise, their time, and their help we'd like to thank the following pro and amateur, classical and contemporary vocalists, classical and non-classical teachers, therapists, scientists, and other voice experts:

Harm K. Schutte M.D., Ph.D. (phoniatrician/ENT-specialist, Groningen Voice Research Lab), Ank Reinders (teacher, author), Monica Millar, Shelly O'Day, Deborah Carter, Sherise Alofs-Parker, Maria Rondèl, Davina Cowan, Alfons Verreijt, Rein Bakker, Angela van Rijthoven, Jaap A. Veldhuizen M.D. (ENT-specialist), Will Vermeer, Jeroen Manuhutu, Hester Noyon, Judith van Elten, Rita Jansen, Marja Oldenhave, Tanya Saw (Zap Mama), Irene van Tol, Ferry Verhoeven, Eric Rutten (TM Audio/Shure), and Dick Lindner (Sennheiser).

About the Author

Journalist and musician **Hugo Pinksterboer**, author and editor of The Tipbook Series has published hundreds of interviews, articles and instrument reviews, and DVD, CD, and book reviews for a variety of international music magazines.

About the Designer

Illustrator, designer, and musician **Gijs Bierenbroodspot** has worked as an art director for a wide variety of magazines and has developed numerous ad campaigns. While searching in vain for information about saxophone mouthpieces, he got the idea for this series of books on music and musical instruments. He is responsible for the layout and illustrations of all of the Tipbooks.

Acknowledgments

Cover photo: René Vervloet
Editors: Robert L. Doerschuk, Michael J. Collins, and Laura Sassano
Proofreaders: Nancy Bishop and Patricia Waddy

Anything missing?

Any omissions? Any areas that could be improved? Please go to www.tipbook.com to contact us. Thanks!

Contents

Introduction

This is a book for novice and advanced singers who want to learn more about their instrument – the singing voice. It doesn't teach you how to sing, but it does help you to get the most out of your vocal instrument, whether you sing classical music, spirituals, grunge, heavy metal, jazz, country, salsa, or any other style of music; whether you sing alone or with others, in a choir, at home, in concert halls, jazz clubs, churches, or anywhere else.

Tipbook Vocals – The Singing Voice has been written in collaboration with classical and non-classical singers and teachers, therapists, and other experts. It presents their in-depth knowledge in a very easy-to-read format. All common terminology is explained, allowing you to easily grasp any other literature on the subject, from magazines to books and Internet publications.

Begin at the beginning

The first three chapters are mainly geared toward untrained and novice singers. They cover singing in general, the basics of the vocal instrument, and tips on learning to sing: Do you need lessons, where to find a teacher, reading music, and practicing. These chapters also provide the basic knowledge you need to read the rest of the book.

Advanced singers

Advanced vocalists can skip ahead to any of the other chapters.

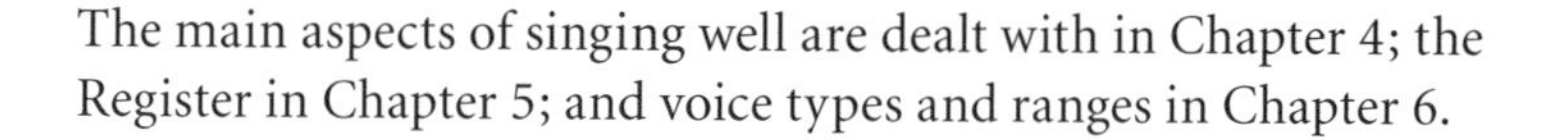

The main aspects of singing well are dealt with in Chapter 4; the Register in Chapter 5; and voice types and ranges in Chapter 6.

Different methods

The terminology used in this book is largely based on what's typically referred to as the classical or bel canto school of singing. Chapter 7 introduces you to some other schools of singing, e.g., the Estill Voice Training System (EVTS) and Complete Vocal Technique (CVT).

Voice care and lyrics

Musical instruments need maintenance; your vocal instrument needs some proper care. The chapter on voice care tells you what you can, should or should not do to keep your voice in prime condition. Another chapter is dedicated to lyrics and how to remember and convey them.

Microphones and effects

Also included is a chapter on microphones and related equipment, providing you with everything you should know to make an informed purchase.

Being prepared

Chapter 12, *Being Prepared*, provides you with helpful hints to reduce audition anxiety and stage fright. After all, singers are often at the center of the audience's attention, and they don't have a physical instrument they can hide behind...

Reading music

As an extra, this new edition of *Tipbook Vocals* includes a chapter on the basics of reading music, showing you how easy it really is.

Glossary

The glossary at the end of the book briefly explains most of the terms you'll come across as a singer. Also included is a complete index of terms. The section *Want To Know More?* provides you additional sources of information. Enjoy!

– Hugo Pinksterboer

See and hear what you read with Tipcodes

www.tipbook.com

In addition to the many illustrations on the following pages, Tipbooks offer you a new way to see – and even hear – what you are reading about.
The Tipcodes that you will come across throughout this book give you access to short movies, soundtracks, and other additional information at www.tipbook.com.

Here is how it works: On page 7 of this book there's a paragraph on how vocal folds (or vocal cords) vibrate. Right above that paragraph it says **Tipcode VOCALS-002**.
Type in that code on the Tipcode page at www.tipbook.com and you will see a short movie that shows you what this looks like. Similar movies and soundtracks are available on a variety of subjects.

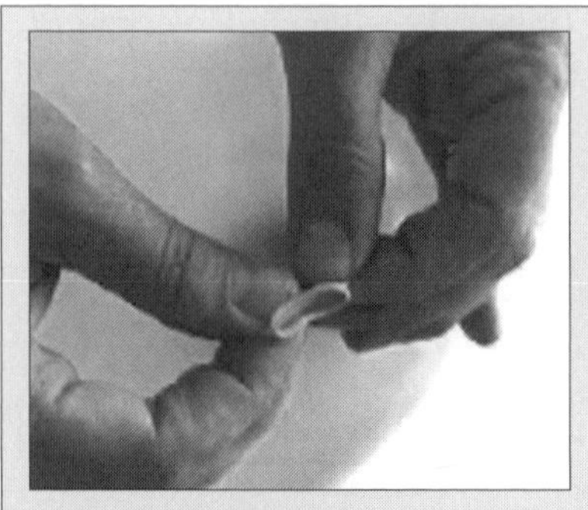

Tipcode VOCALS-002
This Tipcode first shows you how the opening of a balloon can act like a valve, just like your vocal folds. Actual moving vocal folds are also shown.

Enter code, watch movie

You enter the Tipcode below the movie window on the Tipcode page. In most cases, you will then see the relevant images within five to ten seconds. Tipcodes activate a short movie, sound, or both, or a series of photos.

Tipcode list

For your convenience, the Tipcodes presented in this book are also listed on page 212.

Quick start

The Tipcode movies, photo series, and soundtracks are designed so that they start quickly. If you miss something the first time, you

First, make your selection: Tipcode, chords and fingering charts, or the glossary.

The Tipcode window displays videos, fingering charts, chords, or a glossary of the terms used in this book.

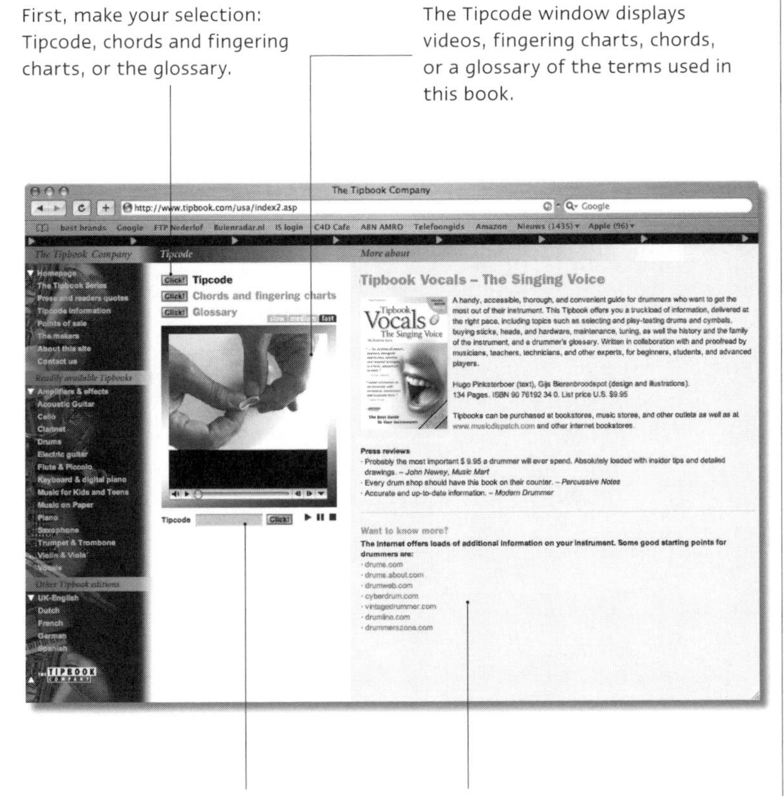

Enter a Tipcode here and click on the button. Want to see it again? Click again.

These links take you directly to other interesting sites.

can of course repeat them. And if it all happens too fast, use the pause button below the movie window.

Plug-ins

If the software you need to view the videos is not yet installed on your computer, you'll automatically be told which software you need, and where you can download it. This software is free. Questions? Check out 'About this site' at www.tipbook.com.

Still more at www.tipbook.com

You can find even more information at www.tipbook.com. For instance, you can look up words in the glossaries of *all* the Tipbooks published to date. There are chord diagrams for guitarists and pianists; fingering charts for saxophonists, clarinetists, and flutists; and rudiments for drummers. Also included are links to most of the websites mentioned in the *Want to Know More?* section of each Tipbook.

1

A Singer?

Singing is one of the world's most popular pastimes. Why? Almost everyone can sing; singing is free; you can sing in pretty much any musical style; you can join choirs and bands, even with little or no training; you can create your own one-piece band; and there's so much more... A chapter on singing and singers, on what makes it fun — and what can make it scary.

The singing voice is the only musical instrument that you don't have to pay for. It's also the only instrument that you can't replace, should you not like it. But you can improve it. You can learn to sing higher notes, improve your tone, develop stamina, and prevent pain and strain — much like learning to play any other musical instrument. And almost everyone can learn to sing in tune!

Easy

The singing voice is an easy access instrument. You can probably sing along to whatever music it is you like — maybe not in perfect pitch, maybe not in perfect time, but well enough to enjoy yourself. And if you're just a bit gifted, you will be able to join a choir, without any training or formal lessons. Any other musical instrument requires serious practice before you can play along to the music you like — let alone join a band.

Personal

The singing voice is the most personal of all instruments. Guitarists, violinists, saxophonists, and other instrumentalists need to work hard to develop a recognizable, personal sound. As a singer, you get one for free. On the other hand, you're not free to choose the sound of your singing voice. You can improve or adjust it to a certain extent, but in the end, you may have a voice that's not perfect for the style of music you would have loved to sing.

Versatile

That said, most people's voices allow them to sing a wide variety of musical styles, and in at least as wide a variety of musical settings, ranging from one-piece bands (just you and your guitar, for example) to hundred-piece choirs.

Entertain a crowd

Most people can sing well enough to enjoy themselves. Unfortunately, not everyone can sing well enough to entertain a crowd. Yet, there are quite a few non-classical vocalists who make millions of dollars with a less-than-perfect voice, according to the critics.

Relaxing and direct

Many singers sing because they find it relaxing. As it requires good breathing, it may have the same effect as yoga, for example.
Singing is also a very direct way to communicate; it's the easiest way to convey a musical message.

Vulnerable

On the downside, singers have to deal with an instrument that's quite vulnerable. Other instruments can't catch colds or infections, they don't suffer if you drink milk or smoke heavily, and they can be played for hours without any ill effect.

Scary

Also, as a singer, you can't hide behind your instrument. You can't blame your instrument if you don't perform well: As a singer, *you* are your instrument. That can be quite scary.

Out front — or in the back

Standing in the front of the stage, which is where singers usually are, can make singing even scarier. But many singers *do* want to be out front. They want to be the most recognizable face in the band. They want the leading role in the opera. If you don't, but you still want to sing, you can sing background vocals, join a choir, or just sing in the privacy of your own home, for example.

Classical and non-classical

There are hundreds of musical styles, and numerous different ways of singing. This Tipbook mainly deals with *classical singing* (opera, art songs, hymns, etc.) and *non-classical* or *contemporary singing* (rock, blues, pop, jazz, gospel, Latin, and so on).

More styles

Of course, there are many more styles of singing, from Chinese opera to the Indian drumming language *konakkol*; from flamenco and Eskimo singing to Japanese and African vocal traditions — and so on.

Singers, vocalists, and instrumentalists

In this book, the words singer *and* vocalist *are used interchangeably for anyone who sings — as an amateur, as a pro, or as anything in between. The word* instrumentalist *is reserved for those who play any other instrument. And both singers and instrumentalists are* musicians.

2

A Quick Tour

The vocal instrument resembles other musical instruments more than you might think. This chapter covers how it basically works, describing the main 'parts' that make up the human voice.

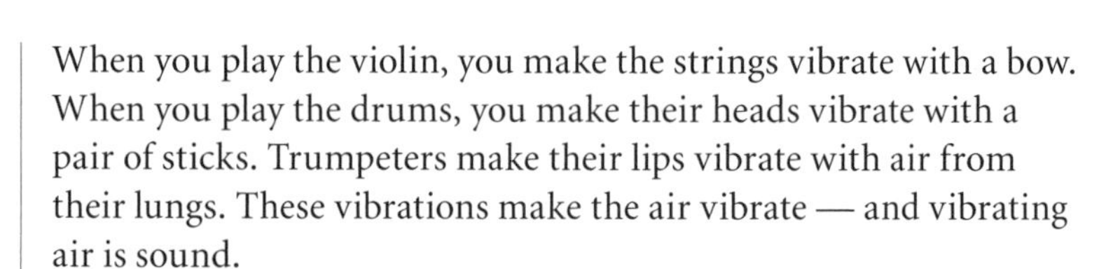

When you play the violin, you make the strings vibrate with a bow. When you play the drums, you make their heads vibrate with a pair of sticks. Trumpeters make their lips vibrate with air from their lungs. These vibrations make the air vibrate — and vibrating air is sound.

Vocal folds

As a singer, you make your *vocal folds* or *vocal cords* vibrate. These folds or cords are two tiny muscles, covered by mucous membrane, located in your throat.
The opening between these muscles is known as the *glottis*. Your vocal folds generate the sound of your voice.

How it works

To roughly understand how this works, close your mouth. Now slowly fill it with air from your lungs. If you keep your lips together just lightly, the air pressure will at one point drive them apart. Then a small puff of air will escape.

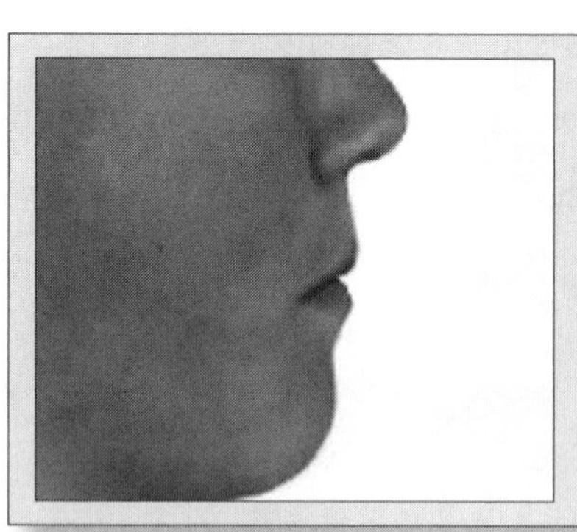

Tipcode VOCALS-001

Tipcode Vocals-001 demonstrates the contents of the paragraph above: fill your mouth with air from your lungs, and let small puffs or air escape.

Cough

You close your mouth by bringing your lips together. Likewise, you can close your glottis by bringing your vocal folds together. To do so, inhale, and act as if you are about to cough — but don't cough.
The closed glottis blocks your air stream. If you concentrate, you can now carefully let a small puff of air escape from between your vocal folds.

Puff, puff, puff

When you speak or sing, this happens all the time: Speaking or singing is letting rapid series of puffs of air from your lungs escape from between your vocal folds.

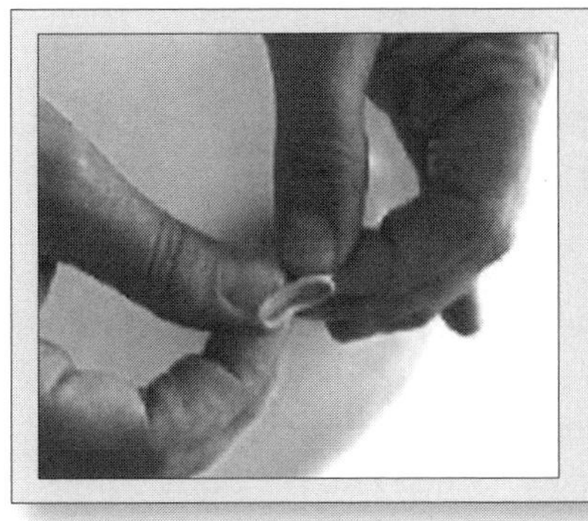

Tipcode VOCALS-002

This Tipcode first shows you how the opening of a balloon can act like a valve, just like your vocal folds. Actual moving vocal folds are also shown.

The human voice

Here's how it works: You build up air pressure from your lungs, and the vocal folds let a puff of air escape; then the folds come together again, new pressure builds up from below — and so on.

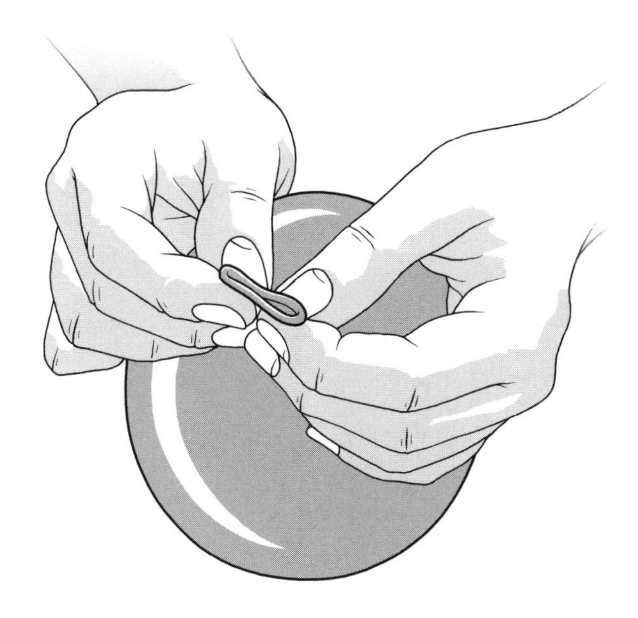

This way, the opening of a balloon acts like a valve, similar to your vocal folds.

This goes so fast that you don't hear separate puffs. What you hear is the human voice.

Balloon

Actually, if you let the air of a balloon escape by stretching the opening between your fingers, something similar happens. The opening of the balloon acts like a valve, just like your vocal folds. It lets the air from the balloon escape in a fast series of 'puffs,' just like your vocal folds do with the air from your lungs.

The lowest note

When a man sings one of the lowest notes he can sing, his glottis opens and closes 66 times per second. In other words, his vocal folds vibrate 66 times per second, and 66 puffs of air escape. He sings a note of 66 hertz, in technical terms. This is a C2, as shown on the piano keyboard below.

C2 is one of the lowest notes of the male voice. Female singers can sing up to an F♯6 – and some even sing higher notes.

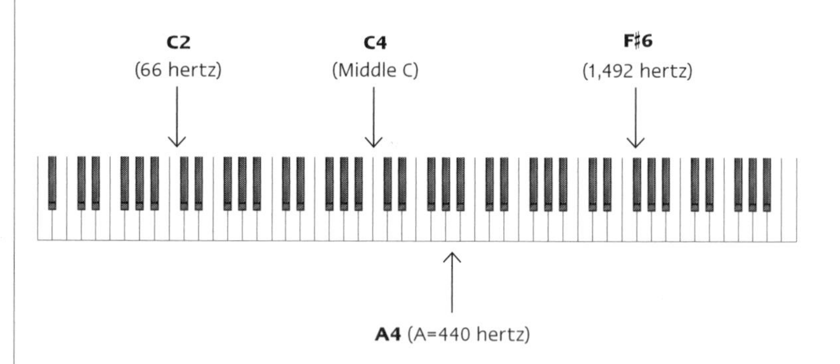

Tipcode VOCALS-003
In Tipcode Vocals-003, the entire range of the human voice is played on a piano.

The highest note
When a female singer sings her highest notes, her vocal folds vibrate some twenty times as fast — up to 1,500 times per second or more!

FOUR PARTS

The vocal folds are one of the four main parts of the vocal instrument. Here are the others.

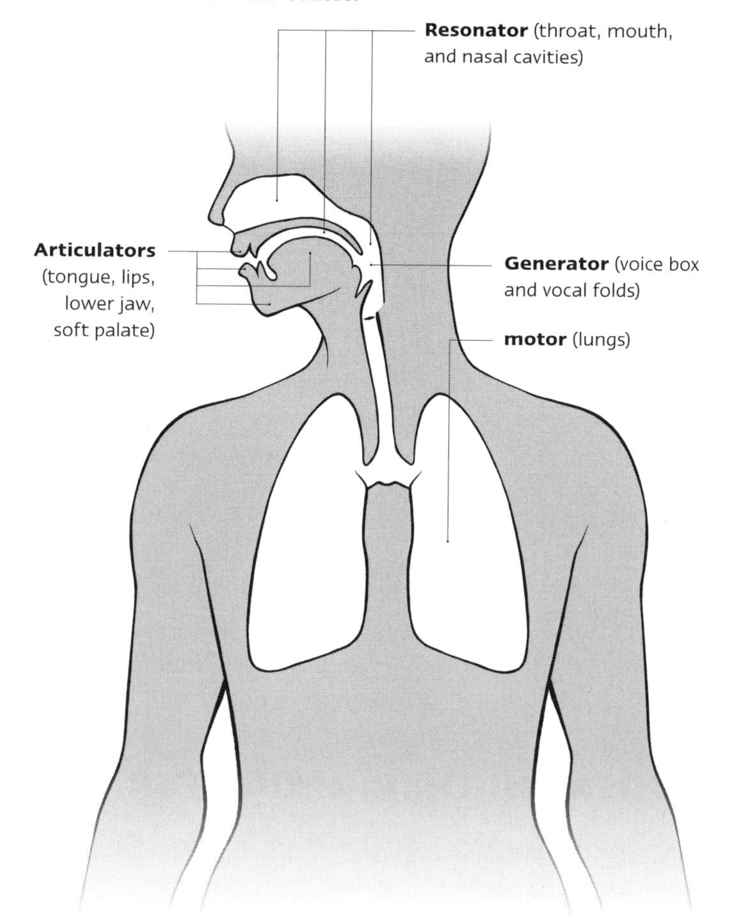

Motor

Your vocal folds use the same 'motor' as trumpeters, saxophonists or other *wind instrument* players do: air. You play these instruments by blowing air into them, set in vibration by the player's lips (trumpet), a reed (sax) or your vocal folds (voice). Basically, the voice is a wind instrument!

Resonator

Your pharynx, mouth, and nasal cavity are like the body of a clarinet, a saxophone, or any other instrument. This is where your voice gets its specific sound or timbre. Together, they're the *resonator* of your vocal instrument, also known as the *vocal tract.*

Jaw, lips, tongue

If you sing an *ah*, and then slide to a *u* as in h*oo*d, then to an *oh*, and an *ee* — you'll notice that you create these and other vowels by changing the position of your lower jaw, lips, and tongue. In technical terms: You change the shape of your resonator. This is known as *articulation.*

Consonants

You use your lower jaw, tongue, lips, soft palate, and other *articulators* to create consonants (B, C, D, F, G, and so on) and most other sounds your voice can produce.

Four parts

So these are the four main 'parts' of your voice: The air from your lungs (1) makes your vocal folds (2) vibrate. The sound generated by the vocal folds is shaped in the resonator (3) by using your articulators (4).

LOUDER, HIGHER, BRIGHTER

You can sing softly and loudly, you can sing high and low notes, and you can make your voice sound brighter or huskier as you please.

Volume

As you sing louder, the movements of your vocal folds become 'edgier', resulting in 'edgier' puffs of air. You don't use more air to sing louder. If you did, you wouldn't be able to sing loud, long notes.

Pitch

As you sing higher or lower notes, the shape and tension of your vocal folds change. When you sing low notes, your vocal folds are thick and slack. The higher the note you're singing, the thinner and tighter they get. When you sing your highest note, your vocal folds are fully stretched, and only their edges vibrate.

Balloon

Actually, what happens with your vocal folds when you sing higher notes is much like what happens if you stretch the opening of the balloon mentioned earlier. The more you stretch it, the higher the pitch gets.

No resonator

The balloon has no resonator. As a result, the sound it makes — escaping air in a fast series of puffs — is very thin. It lacks depth, character, and musicality. If you'd take your vocal folds out of your body, they would produce a very similar, thin sound.

No body

A trumpeter or a sax player can easily demonstrate what the effect of a resonator is. Ask one to play his or her mouthpiece only. All you'll hear is a thin, shallow sound. Now ask the player to attach the instrument (the resonator!) to the mouthpiece. This makes for a musical, *resonant tone.*

Timbre

You use your articulators to create vowels, consonants, and other sounds, but also to influence the timbre of your voice. You can make your voice sound bright, subdued, nasal, or open, simply by positioning your lips or your tongue, for example.

More complicated

The vocal instrument is a lot more complicated than pictured so far. You may not need the following information to sing, but it can be helpful when reading the other chapters.

No Latin

This book doesn't feature in-depth information on, or the Latin names of the dozens of muscles, nerves, and other body parts involved in voice production. If you want to read more about those details, then consult any of the more technical books on singing (see pages 214–216).

VOCAL FOLDS AND VOICE BOX

The vocal folds are often referred to as *vocal cords*. However, they

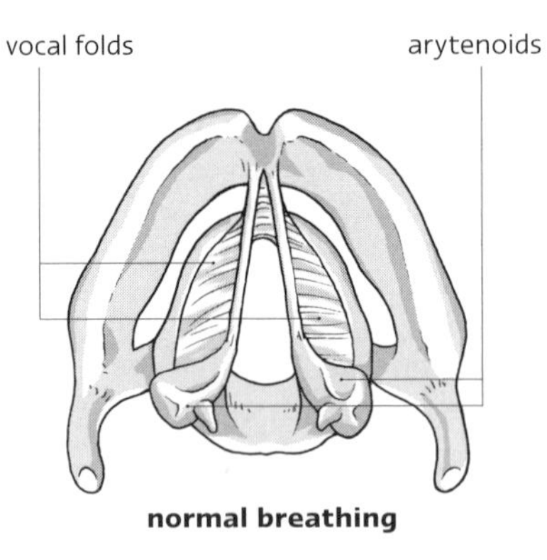

normal breathing

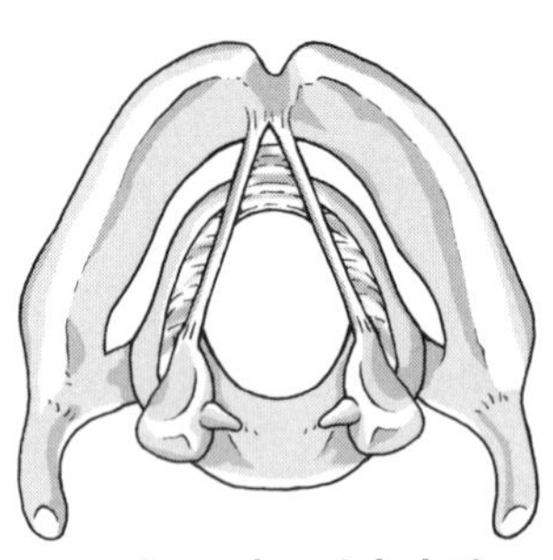

yawning = deep inhalation

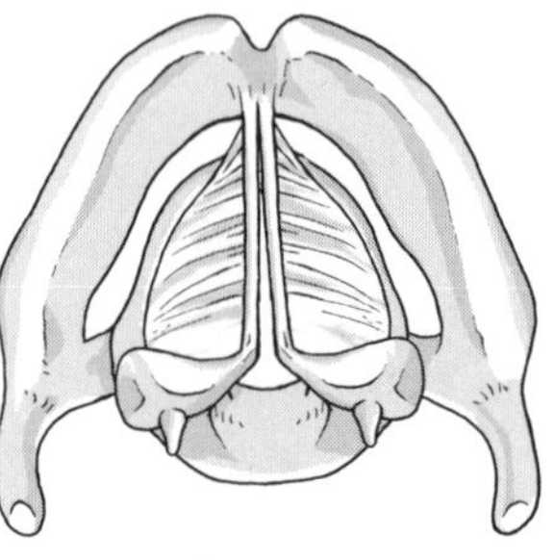

whispering

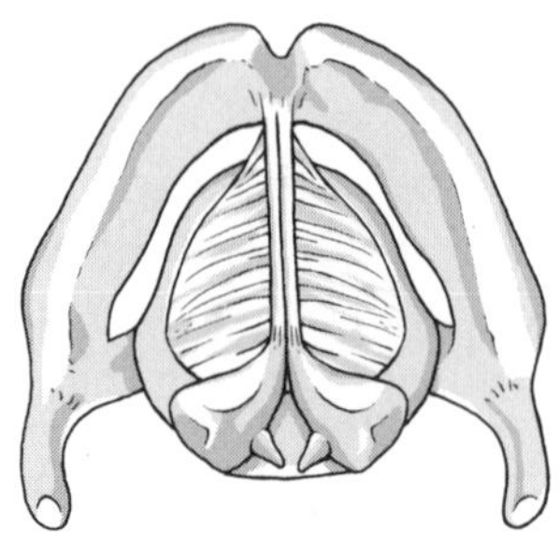

fully closed

don't look like cords, and they don't vibrate like cords or (guitar) strings either.

Muscle and mucosa

Very simply put, vocal folds are muscle tissue covered with mucosa — the same type of mucous membrane that covers the inside of your cheeks.

Short and pale

Your vocal folds are very short — about half an inch to an inch. If they're in good health, they're pale white. You can't check that, unless you have the proper optical instruments.

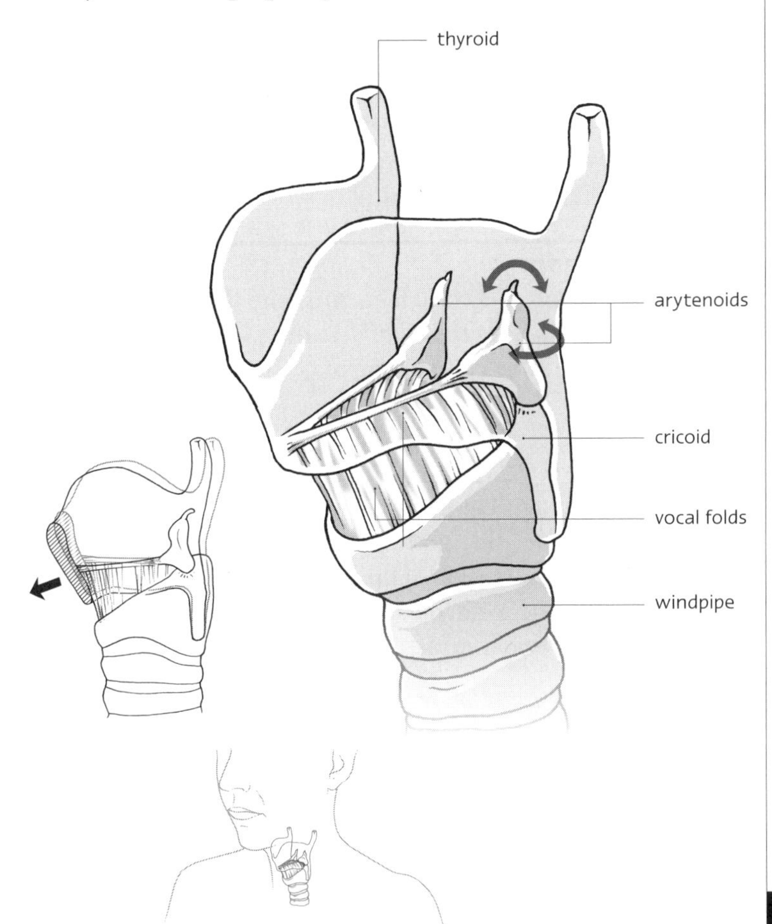

The ring-shaped cricoid sits on top of the flexible windpipe. The thyroid and arytenoids are attached to it so they can move in various ways, adjusting the position of the vocal folds.

Seen from the side: The thyroid can rock forward, stretching the vocal folds.

Open and close

To breathe, your glottis needs to be wide open. To whisper, it needs to be almost closed. To speak or sing, you bring your vocal folds together (*adduction*). And to be able to sing lower and higher notes, their shape has to change — from thick, slack, and short to thin, tight, and long.

Rotating, gliding, moving

The vocal folds can make these and many other movements because they are attached to two small cartilages that can both rotate and glide up and down: the *arytenoids*.

Voice box

The arytenoids are part of the *larynx* or *voice box*, which houses the vocal folds. The larynx is the structure you see moving up and down a man's throat as he swallows. A woman's or a child's voice box isn't that visible — but you can feel it moving up and down if you put your hand on your throat.

From back to front

Inside the voice box, the vocal folds run from the arytenoids, at the back, to the inside of the *thyroid*, at the front.
Men have a more or less pointed thyroid: This is the clearly visible *Adam's apple.*

Rock

The thyroid is attached to the ring-shaped *cricoid* in a way that allows it to rock and glide a little. When the thyroid moves forward, it raises the tension of the vocal folds, which are attached to it. This allows the vocal folds to produce higher notes. The following section briefly explains how this works.

REGISTERS AND THE BREAK

When untrained singers sing from low to high or the other way around, their voices usually 'break' at one point. At that point, the timbre of their voice changes: It's full and dark in the lower range, and quite thin in the higher range.

Tipcode VOCALS-004
Play this Tipcode and you will hear very obvious breaks in a female and a male voice.

Low to high

When singing a *glissando* (a gliding note) from low to high, the thyroid rocks forward at the *break*. This stretches the vocal folds so they can produce higher notes.

High to low

As you sing a glissando from high to low, the thyroid moves backward at one point. This decreases the tension on the vocal folds, allowing them to produce lower, darker notes.

Different vibrations

Below the break, the vocal folds vibrate entirely: Both the muscle tissue and the mucosa are involved. Above the break, only the

Tipcode VOCALS-005
This Tipcode clearly demonstrates the different timbres below and above the break.

edges of the folds vibrate. This makes for two distinctly different timbres.

Registers

These two modes of vibration are referred to as *registers*. Experts — from singers to scientists — often disagree about how many registers there are, and they disagree even more about their names. Also, some singing methods don't speak of registers at all (see Chapter 7).

Modal or chest

The mode for the low notes is known as the *modal register, chest register,* or *heavy register.* The name 'chest register' stems from the vibrations you may feel in your chest when singing low notes.

Light or head

When singing in the higher, *light* register, only the outer edges of the vocal folds vibrate. This is also known as the *head register,* while others call it *falsetto.*

Head register

The term head register or *head voice* stems from the vibrations these higher notes may cause in your head. Others use the term head register for the female high register, and the term falsetto for male singers. Chapter 5 tells you more about registers and their (many!) names.

Using the break

In some styles of music, singers make deliberate use of the break between the registers. A well-known example is yodeling, which involves making quick leaps from one register to another. In most other styles of singing, however, an audible 'break' is undesirable. For more information, again, see Chapter 5.

Passaggio

A friendlier term for the break is *passaggio.* It's where you 'pass'

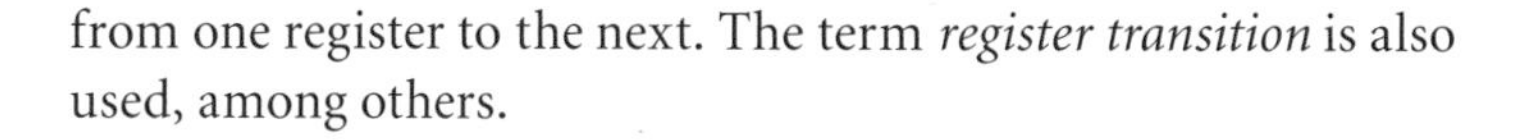

from one register to the next. The term *register transition* is also used, among others.

Men and women

Both men and women have this passaggio in the same part of their range, *i.e.*, between C4 (Middle C) and F4. Both men and women speak at a pitch below this area: You use your chest register for speaking.

Singing

Most male singers, in any style, also sing in their heavy or chest register. Most non-classical female singers do so too. Classical female singers, however, typically sing in the higher register.

Piano or guitar

The illustration on page 85 shows where the passaggio is on a piano keyboard. If you have a guitar at hand: The passaggio of the human voice usually occurs around the pitch of the thin, open E-string (E4).

BREATHING

Singing is often described as *sustained speech*: When you sing, you make vowels, words, or sounds last longer than when you speak. Many aspiring singers need to learn to adapt their breathing so they can support their voices, rather than going flat like a balloon during the first long note. To sing well, you should breathe well.

Breathe in

Good singers breathe in by expanding their belly and sides. When you do so, you flatten your *diaphragm*: That's the large, dome-shaped muscle that separates your lungs from your abdomen. As is flattens down, air rushes into your lungs.

Breathe out

If you let your diaphragm 'snap up' again, you're out of air right

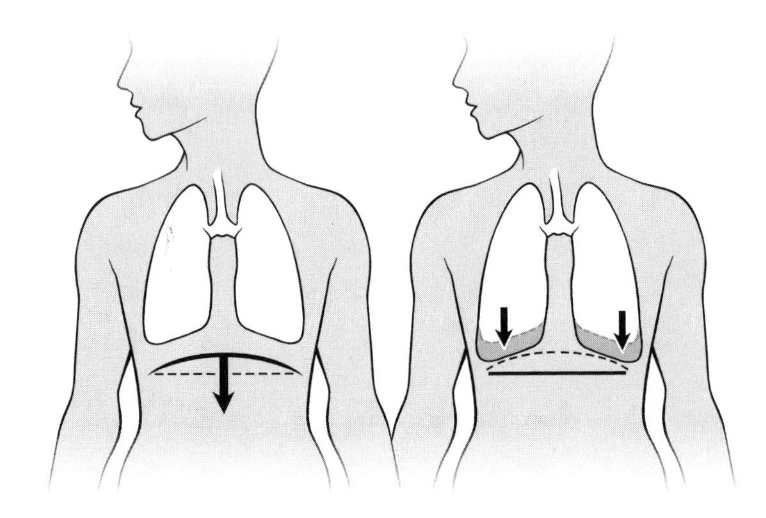

If you expand your belly, your diaphragm flattens down and air rushes into your lungs.

away. In order to be able to sustain your speech you need to keep your diaphragm low and your sides expanded while you exhale, using the air stream to set your vocal folds in motion.

Breath support

By keeping your belly and sides expanded (in other words: by keeping your diaphragm low), you literally support your breath — which is why this technique is known as *breath support*. Singers often have to learn how to consciously apply breath support, though everyone uses it automatically when coughing, for example.

VOICE TYPES

Men's voices sound lower than women's voices. Men typically speak lower than women too. The difference in pitch of their speaking voices is about an *octave*: eight white notes on a piano keyboard.

Lower, darker

Some men have lower, darker voices than others; women all have different voices too. These different voices are classified as *voice types*.

Male voice types

Male singers with very low, dark voices are known as *basses*. Men with relatively light, higher pitched voices are typically referred to as *tenors*. In between are the *baritones*.

Female voice types

The *alto* parts in operas or choirs are sung by women with warm, lower sounding voices. The *sopranos* sing the highest, brightest parts. In between are the *mezzo-sopranos*.

Non-classical singers too?

These classifications are mainly used in the world of classical singing and in choirs. But non-classical singers can benefit from knowing what 'type of voice' they have too: It can help them identify the range and timbre in which they sing most comfortably.

Two to three

Most singers have a range — the musical distance from their lowest to their highest note — of about two to three octaves. The illustration below shows the typical ranges of the voice types mentioned above.

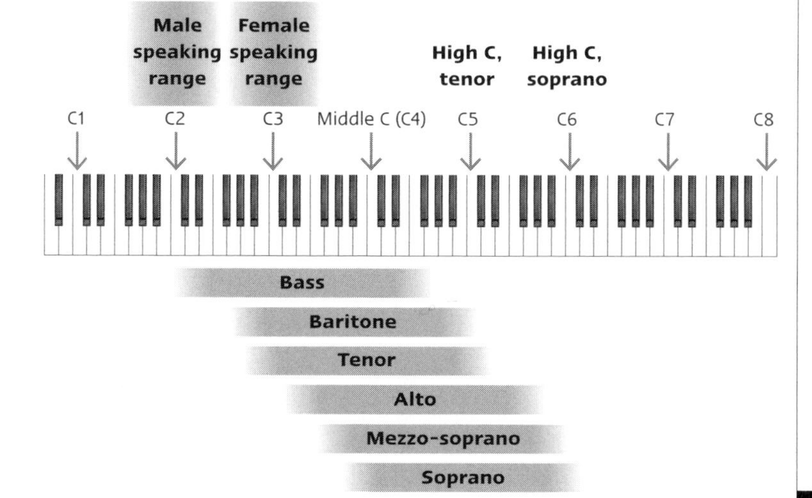

Ranges of the six main types of voice

3

Learning to Sing

Almost everybody can sing — so why take singing lessons? And does it make sense to learn how to read music? This chapter answers those questions and covers subjects such as finding a good teacher, practicing, and practicing aids.

There are various names for the experts who teach singing: vocal teacher, voice teacher, teacher of singing, or singing coach, for example. In this Tipbook, they're all called 'teacher.'

Plenty

Some vocalists sing for years without ever feeling the need for a teacher. Still, there are plenty of reasons why singing lessons can be useful.

Obvious

Sometimes the need for singing lessons is obvious: You run out of breath after a couple of minutes singing; you know you tend to sing out of tune; there's this awful break when switching registers; you can't sing as high as you want to... A teacher can help you solve those problems.

Too late

Many singers don't visit a teacher until something goes wrong — if it hurts when they sing or even when they swallow, when they repeatedly lose their voices, when their stamina is reduced, and so on. A teacher can remedy some of these problems, but medical help may be required too. Good voice lessons can help prevent problems.

Consistent quality

Pop singers often start taking on a teacher or coach after they've signed with a major record company: Their newly acquired fame demands consistent quality in spite of irregular sleep hours, extensive concert touring, excessive talking for interviews, and so on.

Never

On the other hand, non-classical singers often hesitate to take singing lessons because they're afraid it will spoil their (rough, rugged, raw, raucous, 'non-classical') trademark sound. Or they're afraid that good singing technique might spoil their expressiveness. It doesn't need to, however. Good voice lessons can help preserve your personal sound *and* your voice, make singing less painful, and prevent possible damage.

Grunge

True: There are many teachers who thoroughly disapprove of the way grunge, punk, and many other types of singers use their vocal instrument. But others don't: They will help you to produce those growling sounds as safely as possible. And if they don't think your voice is suited for that way of singing, they'll tell you.

Worse at first

If you've been singing for a long time, lessons can make your singing voice break down at first. Why? Because untrained singers often use power and strain to compensate for a lack of technique. Removing the strain can be like removing the foundation of the voice — but you may have to, in order to develop a new, healthier, and more effective vocal technique.

One instrument

As a singer, the only instrument you will ever have is the one you were born with. The only way to make it sound better is to learn how to control it. The only way to make it last longer is to use it as well as you can. Lessons can help you do so.

Someone else's voice

Many rock guitarists preferably buy the same guitar their idol uses — just as aspiring rock singers often try to sing like their heroes. If that doesn't suit your voice, you may damage it. Singing lessons help in finding out what you can and cannot do with your instrument.

Range

Singing lessons can help you add a few higher or lower notes to your range and help ensure you consistently hit the extreme notes of your range.

Volume

Singing lessons can help you sing louder without strain and pain, but also to sing very softly yet clearly. In other words: Singing lessons can definitely increase your *dynamic range.*

Articulation

If you want the audience to understand what you're singing about, and if you want to be able to produce a variety of timbres, you need to articulate well. Good teachers help you do so.

And everything else

And of course, singing lessons also help you develop breath control, posture, practice routines, stamina, presentation, and everything else that can make you a better singer.

Weeks, months, years?

How long do you need to take lessons? As long as you feel your voice isn't ready for what you want to use it for. Some benefit from as little as ten lessons to solve a specific problem; others spend four years of lessons before finding the right teacher, and then stay with that teacher for another few years.

AGE AND SINGING

You can learn to sing at almost any age. And if you sing well, your vocal instrument can last for many decades.

Children

Most children's voices sound very much alike — bright and high-pitched. When puberty comes, things change.

Boys

For boys, this change occurs a lot faster than for girls. Usually around age twelve or thirteen, the male larynx and vocal folds start to grow rapidly, giving access to a new, lower register: the chest register. In this phase, boys often have a hard time controlling their vocal folds, which often don't grow in accordance with the other parts of the vocal instrument.

Leaps

The result of this sudden, irregular growth is a voice that leaps from one register to the other. This involuntary yodeling may last quite a while. The mutation from a boy's voice to an adult male voice typically takes one to two years, between ages twelve and fifteen. The adult male voice is about an octave lower than a boy's voice.

Girls

The mutation of the female voice can last a couple of years, usually from the ages twelve to sixteen until ages eighteen or twenty. In those years, the growth of the larynx and vocal folds may result in a breathy voice, as the vocal folds don't fully close. Some female singers tend to continue singing and speaking this way, which may result in nodules (see page 129) and other symptoms.

How much

So while the male voice drops about an octave, the adult female voice is about a third to a fifth lower than a girl's voice: It's a much smaller difference, and it's a much more gradual process too.

Continue?

Many experts agree that adolescents can safely continue singing throughout their vocal mutation. Extra guidance may be recommended, however, especially when young singers perform often, or in demanding situations.

Getting older

The adult voice changes over the years. It becomes darker, and often more expressive and mature. Later on brightness decreases, the range is reduced (high notes getting harder to sing) or lowered, vibrato tends to deepen and slow down, and it may become harder to sing very softly, to project well, or to overcome the dreaded passaggio. Whether that's a problem may depend on the style of music you're singing. Most classical singers have to end their professional careers around age fifty (female singers) or sixty (male singers), though there are vocalists who continue singing professionally for many more years.

WHICH TEACHER?

Finding a good teacher may take you a while. First of all, you need to feel comfortable with your prospective teacher, as he or she will deal with some very personal issues: your breathing, your posture, and the sound of your voice.

Sing all day long

As you will see in this book, there are many different ideas about how the vocal instrument works. Likewise, there are many different and often conflicting ideas about how to explain and teach singing — and no one knows who's right. For many singers, amateurs and aspiring pros alike, the best teachers are the ones that make you feel like you want to sing all day long.

Non-classical

Can non-classical singers benefit from the lessons of a classical singer? Sometimes they can, and there are classically trained teachers who teach singers in any style with great success. But that doesn't mean that good classical technique would necessarily be the best basis for any other style of music.

Male or female

Some teachers believe that, after a basic vocal education, male singers need male teachers, and female teachers should teach female singers. Others don't. Many experts feel that good teachers can teach anyone to sing, male or female, beginner or advanced.

Specialized teachers

Still, you may want to find a special teacher for special purposes. Consult a bass singer if you have a bass voice. Find a jazz singer if you want to sing jazz. And find out about gospel singing from a gospel singer. The basics of good singing in any style, though, are more alike than some say.

Different teachers

Teachers also differ in what they concentrate on. For example, some focus on the physiological or technical aspects of singing (where it all starts), while others concentrate on tone, presentation, and interpretation (where it all should go). Oftentimes, the best teachers are the ones who have the ability to offer you a wealth of information as well as the ability to use different approaches. Imagery, if technique doesn't work for you. Physiology, if imagery doesn't work. And so on.

Different techniques

There are various singing methods that teachers may use. Some examples are:

- *EVTS (Estill Voice Training System)*
- *CVT (Complete Vocal Technique)*
- *SLS (Speech Level Singing)*

A brief rundown of these and other singing methods or techniques is provided in Chapter 7.

Questions, questions

Here are some other questions you may ask when trying to find a teacher.

- Is an **introductory lesson** included? This is a good way to find out how well you get on with the teacher.
- Is the teacher interested in taking you on as a student even if you are doing it just **for the fun of it**, or will he or she expect you to practice at least three hours a day?
- Do you have to make a large investment in method books right away, or is the **course material provided**?
- Can you **record your lessons**, so that you can listen again to how you sounded and what was said when you get home?

Finding a teacher

Looking for a private teacher? Music stores may have teachers on their staff, or be able to refer you to one. You can also consult your local Musicians' Union, or the choir director at a high school. Check the classified ads in newspapers, in music magazines, or on supermarket bulletin boards, and consult the *Yellow Pages* or the Internet (see page 217). You may also look for a teacher among faculties at nearby music schools, high schools, and colleges. Professional private teachers will usually charge between twenty-five and seventy-five dollars per hour. Some make house calls, for which you'll pay extra.

Group or individual lessons

While most students take individual lessons, you can also try group lessons if that's an option in your area. Private lessons are more expensive but can be tailored exactly to your needs.

Collectives

You may want to check whether there are any teacher collectives or music schools in your vicinity. These organizations often offer extras such as choirs or ensembles you can join in various styles and at various levels.

READING MUSIC

Many contemporary singers don't read music — and there are classical singers that don't either, though very few. Does it make sense to learn to read music, as a singer?

Up or down, short or long

If you know how to read music, you don't have to rely on your memory for every note you sing: You can use sheet music. And even if you can't read perfectly, the written notes will remind you of the direction of the melody (pitch going up or down, a bit or a lot), and of the rhythm (how long the notes last).

More of a musician

If you know how to read music, it'll be easier to communicate with musicians who do too. You know what they mean when they're talking about B-flat minor, transposition, or a triplet feel. That can make you more of a musician, rather than 'just a singer.'

Songbooks

The ability to read music also gives you access to the many songbooks available, so you'll no longer need to listen to a song numerous times before you can sing it.

Exercises

Also available are books with special vocal or ear training exercises, and many books on singing include valuable exercises and examples in musical notation.

Not that hard

Reading music isn't that hard to learn. Making the written notes sound at their proper pitches is a bit harder for singers than it is for most instrumentalists, though. A pianist, for example, just presses the appropriate C-key when the chart shows a C. And a saxophonist knows which keys to press for each written note. As a singer, you don't have keys: You have to 'hear' the written note in your mind to be able to sing it at its proper pitch.

Reading music isn't that hard to learn.

A home keyboard

A basic home keyboard can help you in this process. It allows you to play the melody notes in your sheet music, so you can then sing what you hear. Learning to play this instrument to this extent is a matter of weeks at the most.

Chapter 13

For your convenience, this edition of *Tipbook Vocals* comes with a chapter that teaches you — or helps you refresh your memory on — the basics of reading music. This chapter, *Reading Music*, is based on *Tipbook Music on Paper – Basic Theory* (see page 223).

PRACTICING

Regular practice helps you develop your voice, which increases control, power, stamina, pitch, and helps you extend and maintain your range.

How long?

How long you need to practice depends on what you want to achieve. (Aspiring) professionals may spend hours each day on various practice routines. For less ambitious singers, half an hour a day is usually enough to steadily progress. As singing half an hour nonstop is more than most voices can handle, it's best to divide your practicing routine up into two or more shorter sessions.

Exercises

There are many different singing exercises.

- Humming and *lip trills* help to warm up the voice.
- *Vocalizing* is — originally — singing without words, concentrating on various aspects such as breath, tone, rhythm, and evenness throughout the range.
- *Messa di voce* (singing a tone from soft to loud, and back; see page 67) helps develop breath support, tone, and dynamics, among other attributes.
- Sustaining long notes can help to increase your *breath support*, and so can singing short notes with one breath, pushing each one out with the diaphragm and stomach muscles (ba-ba-ba).
- There are many more types of exercises, ranging from exercises that help you improve articulation or *ear-training* exercises that

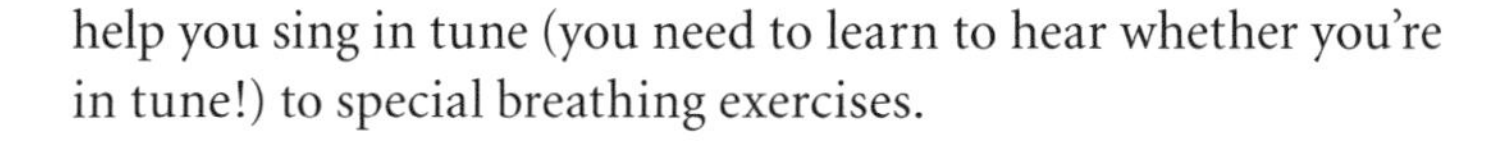

help you sing in tune (you need to learn to hear whether you're in tune!) to special breathing exercises.

Warming up

Warming up the voice is an important element of practicing. If you don't have a regular practice schedule, at least try to discipline yourself to warm up your voice before you sing anything. It will make you sing easier and sound better, and it will help to extend and maintain your range, and to prevent symptoms (see pages 118–120).

Classical and non-classical

Many vocal exercises are essentially the same for every singer, as singers in different styles often use the same basic skills. Special exercises have been developed for special vocal styles, from metal to yodeling, and some teachers will create or adapt exercises for the specific way you sing, or for the things you're working on.

In private

Vocal exercises sometimes require you to produce sounds that you may not want others to hear ('chewing vowels', for example, or glides). If you have a place to practice where no one else can hear you, you don't need to worry about singing out of tune either.

The neighbors

The singing voice can easily sound louder than most other acoustic instruments! If your singing bothers neighbors or housemates, it may be enough to simply agree to fixed practice times. Alternatively, you may try to insulate a room or have that done for you, or find another place to practice.

Accompaniment

You can sing and practice singing just by yourself — but it's often more fun to have some kind of accompaniment.

Practice tapes

First of all, many singers use practice tapes, CDs, or similar media that offer a variety of practice routines that you can sing along with. Guitarists and pianists can also accompany themselves!

Sing along

Singing along to regular CDs, or to the radio, is another option, but you'll always hear the voice of the 'real' singer along with your own.
Alternatively, there are special recordings of the original music without the singing voice, or they have the vocals on the left channel, and the band on the right. To sing along with just the band, turn the balance control of your amp to the right.

Karaoke and voice-killers

You can also use karaoke CDs, or try to remove the singer's voice from a CD by using a voice killer or voice remover, available in hardware (a small box with electronics) or software (a computer program) versions.

MIDI files

Thousands of popular songs are available as MIDI *files. You can play these computer files on most home keyboards, or on computers that have a sound card and the appropriate software. These digital orchestras or bands may not sound as good as real musicians, but they're very flexible and always ready to play, night and day.*

Software

If you have a computer with a sound card, you can purchase software that allows you to program your own virtual 'band.' You can choose the instruments, the style, and the tempo; then you type in the chord sequences, and press Play. Provided you have the right equipment, you may be able to record yourself singing along to the music too. You can also use your computer for ear-training. There's a variety of low-priced ear-training software available.

Internet

The Internet has a lot to offer singers, ranging from MIDI files to the lyrics of many popular songs in a wide variety of musical styles. Besides this, the Internet offers various informative sites (see pages 216–218), singing lessons, practice routines, ear-training courses, and much more.

Video

You can also use instructional videos and DVDs to help you become a better singer — but it goes without saying that neither video lessons nor the Internet can replace real teachers.

The first time

Not too many people like the sound of their voice when they first hear it on a recording. Why? This is mainly because you aren't used to hearing yourself the way other people do. To hear a little bit of what others hear, you can cup your hand(s) behind your ear(s), catching some of the sound that leaves your mouth.

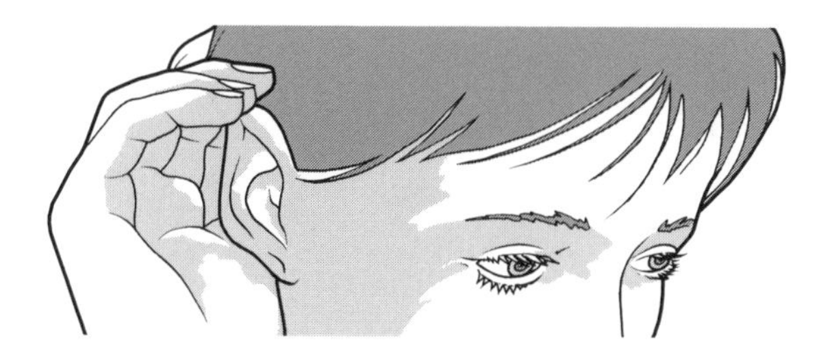

Cup your hand behind your ear...

Record yourself

The best way to keep in touch with how you really sound, however, is to record yourself. Record your lessons, record your practice sessions, record the choir or band with which you sing. Even a basic cassette recorder with a built-in microphone will do for this purpose. Better equipment (a minidisc player with a separate microphone, for instance) is more expensive, but the recordings are usually more enjoyable to listen to and they can be more instructive as well.

4

Singing Well

To a country vocalist, singing well doesn't mean the same as to an operatic singer, a blues shouter, or a Broadway-style belter. Still, so many things are important to almost every singer, in almost any style, at any level. Knowing more about these subjects can help you to understand and extend the possibilities of your voice.

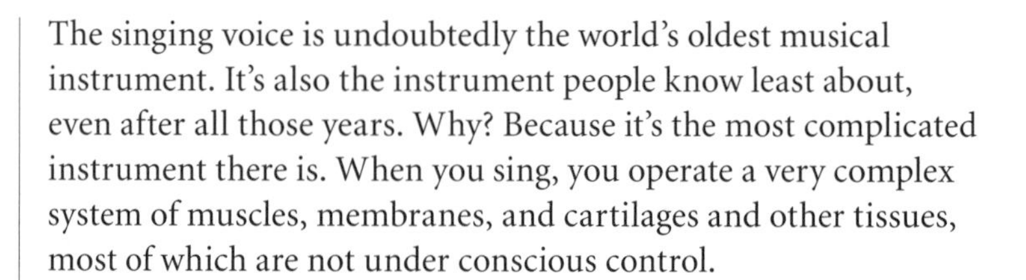

The singing voice is undoubtedly the world's oldest musical instrument. It's also the instrument people know least about, even after all those years. Why? Because it's the most complicated instrument there is. When you sing, you operate a very complex system of muscles, membranes, and cartilages and other tissues, most of which are not under conscious control.

Which muscles

You can make a guitar sound brighter by playing the strings with a plastic pick, rather than using your fingertips. You can make your voice sound brighter too, but you can't tell someone how by telling him which muscles to use.

Imagery

This is why teachers often use imagery to tell you what they mean. You have to place your voice behind your eyes, for example, or they suggest that you sing from your neck, or that you let your voice 'bounce' against your palate, or that you pretend to sing through a hole in the wall…

More sense, no sense

Some of these images make more sense than others. Some are close to how your vocal instrument really works; others aren't at all. But as long as they help to create the desired effect without damaging your voice, they can't hurt.

Open or tight

The meaning of 'singing well' largely depends on the style of music you're singing. An example: In most Western styles of singing, you need to 'open your throat' to sound good. In other styles of singing, however, you need to tighten your throat to produce the desired effect.

Hazardous for some

Likewise, techniques that are considered extremely hazardous for the voice in one style have been used for many years in other styles of singing — without a single problem. And while most singers shouldn't drink milk shortly before their performance, others always do.

Who's right?

All of this helps explain why there are so many conflicting stories and points of view on the subject of singing. This book doesn't tell you who is right or how it really works, if only because no one knows it all. It does tell you what various experts think about the main subjects.

Sing well

This may help you find your own ways to improve and understand your singing voice, allowing you to sing well — to be able to use your voice in a way that you can sing whatever you want to sing, with the range and the volume you need, without hurting your vocal instrument.

Classical or non-classical

This book mainly deals with classical and non-classical or contemporary Western styles of singing. These two large categories are quite alike in many ways, as you'll see elsewhere in this chapter, yet there are some major differences between them.

- Classical singers need a certain **minimum range** to perform the pieces that are available. Many non-classical careers have been built on voices that span little more than an octave — and most popular songs can easily be performed within such a small range.
- The way classical singers sing is often considered unnatural: Their singing voice sounds different from their **natural speaking voice**. Non-classical singers sound much more natural.
- Classical singers are supposed to have **an even timbre** along their entire range. Non-classical singers often deliberately stress the different timbres of their natural registers. Likewise, the **break** or **passaggio** should not be heard in classical music, but there are non-classical styles of singing in which it is used as an effect or technique (*e.g.*, yodeling).
- Classical singers have to learn to **project their voice** to make themselves heard. Non-classical singers use microphones, which allow them to be heard even when singing as softly as they can — or even to build a successful career on a 'small' voice.

- In classical singing, your **timbre** is sometimes considered more important than the lyrics you sing. In non-classical singing, it's usually the other way around.
- In non-classical music, you can sound **breathy**, **hoarse**, **rugged**, **gritty**, **hollow**, **nasal**, or **tight-throated** — and still be successful. As a classical singer, you can't.
- In classical music, the standards for '**singing well**' are much tighter than in non-classical music: Your timbre, your control over your vocal instrument, and your range have to meet certain conditions in order to 'sing well.'

Versatility

Some people have extremely versatile voices. They can learn to sing whatever they want. Others have restrictions. You may have a voice that's simply unsuitable for classical music, or for rugged rock & roll, or for melodic pop. If you insist on singing in those styles anyway, chances are you'll hurt your instrument. A good teacher can help you find out which styles of music best suit your voice.

THIS CHAPTER

This chapter continues with sections on various physical aspects of singing. First are some of the conditions for good singing: breathing, and breath support (page 42); posture (page 44); what (not) to do with your throat (45), your mouth (47), your tongue (48), and your voice box (49). The section on overtones (page 51) offers essential information to be able to fully understand the sections on timbre and resonance (54), and on formants and the singer's formant (62). The following sections deal with some other subjects you can learn to control in order to improve your singing: volume (65), singing in tune (68), articulation (74), the onset or attack (78), and vibrato (80).

BREATHING

The best way to breathe for singers is basically the best way to breathe in everyday life — and it's the way newborn babies breathe. What is good breathing, should you use your nose, your mouth, or both, and how do you prevent running out of breath and noisy breathing?

Large bowl

Well-trained singers use their diaphragm when they breathe, as explained in Chapter 2. When you exhale, this muscle relaxes and takes on the shape of a large bowl, bottom up. To inhale, you flatten your diaphragm. Your belly expands, and air enters the lungs.

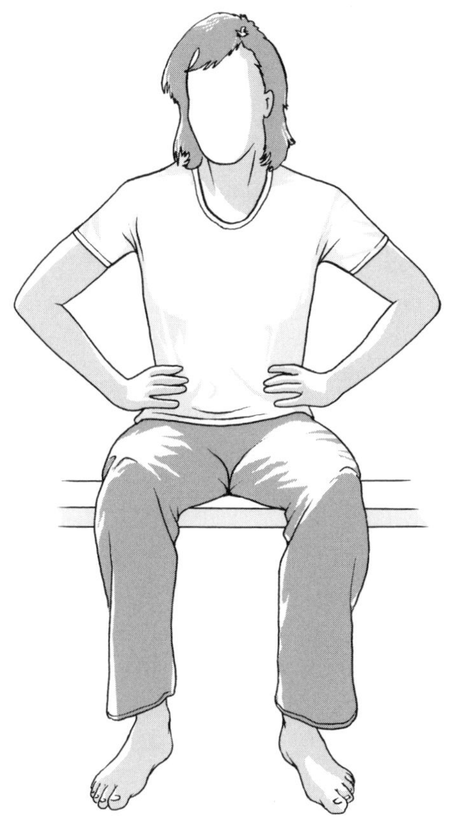

Hold your waist, thumbs in your back, and feel how your belly, sides, and back expand.

Belly breathing

Because of the expanding belly this is known as *belly breathing* or *abdominal breathing*. Your belly is not the only part that expands: Your sides and back expand as well. If you hold your waist with both hands, thumbs in your back, you can clearly feel they do.

Book

An easy way to experience belly breathing is to lie on the floor with a large book on your stomach. Take deep breaths as you watch the book slowly rise and fall.

Rib cage

Often, singers also use their ribs to inhale, expanding their rib cage. This combined breathing technique is known as *costal-abdominal breathing* (*costa* is *rib*). It allows you to breathe efficiently and to carefully control the air stream that goes out, energizing your vocal folds.

> ### *Your shoulders*
>
> *Untrained singers — and many non-singers — often tend to breathe very superficially. They use the upper part of their lungs only, raising their shoulders when they inhale. This type of shallow, upper-chest breathing doesn't supply sufficient air for singing longer phrases. It also makes it harder to relax your larynx and other parts of your vocal instrument, and it can't be controlled as accurately as costal-abdominal breathing.*

How much?

Too much air is as bad as too little air. If you breathe in too deeply, chances are that the superfluous air escapes while you sing (making your voice sound breathy), or that you use tension to prevent the excessive air from flowing out, which doesn't do your vocal performance any good either: You'll probably sound pinched. Singing well is not about breathing deeply, but about breathing well.

Incomplete closure

A breathy tone can also be due to an incomplete closure of the glottis, with air leaking out. This can result in vocal nodules and other problems (see page 129).

Breathy tone

For non-classical singers, a breathy tone isn't bad per se, by the way. For some singers it's their trademark; others use it occasionally. When they do so properly, there's no risk involved. This is mainly a matter of properly controlling the opening of the glottis, rather than letting air escape involuntarily because the vocal folds can't close the glottis correctly over its entire length.

Tipcode VOCALS-006

A breathy tone can be very effective, as you can hear in this Tipcode.

Too little air

If you run out of air very quickly, you're probably using too much when you sing. In most cases, breathing deeper is not the solution. Breathing better and using breath support is.

Timing

You can also run out of air because of bad timing: Singing requires that you plan your breaths throughout a song. Many singers make small marks on their lyric sheets to indicate the best places to take either a quick catch breath or a long breath.

Nose or mouth?

Some singers are nose breathers; others consider themselves strictly mouth breathers. Most singers seem to use both entries,

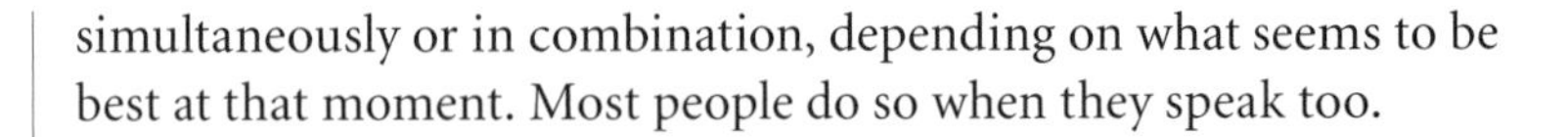

simultaneously or in combination, depending on what seems to be best at that moment. Most people do so when they speak too.

The mouth

Breathing through the mouth takes less time, and if you need to take in breath quickly, it's the only noiseless way. It also helps to lower the larynx and widen the throat, and it enhances belly breathing. However, it dries your mouth, so you may need to drink more, and mouth breathing doesn't offer any protection against airborne pollution.

The nose

Nose breathing offers some protection against dry air, smoke, and other types of air pollution. But it encourages shallow breathing, using just your upper chest. Also, it's hard to get a full breath using your nose only, unless you have a lot of time to spare.

Noiseless breathing

Inhaling through the mouth should be absolutely noiseless. If it isn't, your glottis isn't fully open, and air rushes along the edges of your vocal folds. Want to check? Open your mouth, then breathe in and out, first with a gasping sound and then without it. You switch from gasping to non-gasping by varying the width of the glottis. If you can't get rid of the gasping sound, you can't separate your vocal folds far enough. Ask a teacher for special exercises.

BREATH SUPPORT

Good breathing doesn't do you any good without breath support. If you don't support your breath, you'll run out of air in no time. Proper breath support is also essential for your timbre, your loudness, and pitch control, for example.

Keep it low

If you don't know what breath support is, you may want to try the following. First inhale by expanding your belly, lowering your diaphragm. Put your hands in your sides and feel them expand too. Now hold your breath, but don't block it by either closing your vocal folds (as if you were to say 'air'), lowering your velum (the soft palate; as if you were to say 'go'), using your tongue (as you would when saying 'tea'), or closing your mouth. Instead, hold your breath by *keeping your diaphragm low*: That's what's known as breath support, *air support*, or *abdominal support.*

A belt

You can also put a belt around your waist, at belly height. If you inhale using your diaphragm, the belt will feel tighter. Now exhale — singing or silently — but maintain some tension on the belt. Again, that's breath support.

Sit down

If you have a hard time feeling what's actually going on as you do this exercise, you may want to try it again sitting down, so you can concentrate on your torso only.

Control

Breath support is not just about ensuring that you don't run out of air. It's also about controlling the pressure you build up under your glottis (the *subglottic pressure*) and about balancing it against the closure of the vocal folds. This helps control loudness, but also timbre and pitch.

Tightened throat

Without breath support, you may tend to tighten your throat to prevent air from rushing out, resulting in a pinched sound. You may also tend to use too much tension and develop symptoms in your neck, lower jaw, and tongue.

Sustaining pitch

If you can hit a note in tune but have problems sustaining the pitch, that's probably due to poor breath support. Without proper breath support, you may also have problems extending your range and stamina.

Breathy tone

Quite a few famous pop singers don't have proper breath support. When singing softly, they sound breathy because uncontrolled air escapes. Only when they sing loud — using all the air they have — does their tone become clear and focused.

POSTURE

Good singing requires good breathing, and both require good posture. Your voice benefits from being supported by your entire body, not just the parts that seem to be directly involved.

An expert

Good posture has to do with standing erect in a relaxed way, as if you're pulled up lightly by the top of your head, with neck and torso well-aligned, feet slightly apart, maybe one slightly in front of the other, knees not overstretched, and without using any muscles you shouldn't use. Unfortunately, doing all of this still doesn't guarantee you're doing it right. Only an expert (a good teacher, a voice coach, a physical expert) can tell you.

Natural?

The posture that feels natural to you is not always good. A good singing posture may even feel unnatural at first, just like opening your mouth wide enough for singing.

Music stand

As a choir member, you may have to use sheet music. If so, try using a music stand. Holding the sheet music yourself may constrain your neck and shoulders, or you may tend to tilt your head forward, constricting your throat.

Sit

In some choirs, the singers sit. Singing guitarists and keyboard players often play sitting down too, and singing drummers and pianists always do. If you have to sing sitting down, make sure that your diaphragm has as much working space as if you were standing up. In other words, you shouldn't sit too low. If you play an instrument and use a microphone, make sure the microphone doesn't interfere with your posture. If it does, consider using a headset (see page 149).

Move

Even if you dance or move around a lot when you sing, good posture is as important as it is when you stand or sit still. One of the main problems for singing dancers is breath control, and even famous singers are known to sing terribly out of tune when dancing simultaneously. This problem is often solved by lip-syncing (not just in video clips, but 'live' too), though some singers prefer to practice singing in tune while jogging, for example.

OPEN THROAT

In non-classical literature, you'll often read about the need for an open throat. An open throat, which is necessary to produce an open, non-constricted sound, is a matter of complete relaxation. You don't have muscles to open or widen your throat; you only have muscles to tighten it.

Tipcode VOCALS-007
This is Angela singing identical notes with a tight throat and an 'open' throat: The difference is obvious.

Yawn or bite

Your throat automatically widens when you yawn: Your larynx is lowered, and your glottis opens. The same usually happens when you're about to take a bite from an apple, or when you're genuinely surprised. Again, a teacher can help you further if this doesn't make things clear.

Don't push it

Some singers tend to force their throat open. The resulting sound is often compared to singing with a hot potato in your mouth. There are well-known singers who use that type of sound as their trademark, so it's not bad *per se* — as long as the extra tension doesn't translate into pain, fatigue, or other symptoms, and as long as you don't sing classical music.

Tight throat

Singing with a tighter throat doesn't need to be bad either. Plenty of Western pop singers have built a career on a guttural, 'tight throat' timbre. And *overtone singers* in Tuva, Bulgaria, Vietnam, and other countries tighten their throat so much that the fundamental pitch of their vocal folds is strongly reduced, thus bringing out the whistling sound of the overtones only (see page 51).

Tipcode VOCALS-008
This Tipcode demonstrates the intriguing sound of overtone singing.

Dangerous?

Is singing with such a tight throat dangerous for the vocal instrument? Probably not: Overtone singers can have long, long careers.

Grunting

To grunt, you also tighten your throat a little. The resulting sound incorporates your *false vocal folds*. These folds are located just above the 'regular' vocal folds. Vocalists in various non-classical styles have used or still use these false or *ventricular vocal folds*, from the late jazz singer and trumpeter Louis Armstrong to pop singers and death metal singers.

Detrimental

Many — classically trained and other — experts state that singing this way is detrimental to your voice. Is it? There are plenty of singers who've shown the opposite, and some of them have been around for many decades. Specialized teachers can help you grunt and use other vocal effects without hurting your vocal instrument (see Chapter 7).

YOUR MOUTH

Using your voice to the max usually requires that you open your mouth quite a bit further than you normally do. This may feel awkward at first. If it does, just watch some great singers singing, and see that it doesn't look that weird at all.

Don't push it

Relaxation is the key word, again. You shouldn't force your mouth open, but just let it go. Singing too widely can be just as big a

Smile

A smile tends to add brightness to your sound. In the old days, castratos (see page 167) sang with a smile, covering their upper teeth. Today, some schools of contemporary singing promote a light, 'inner' smile to enhance your timbre. Try the effect by singing the vowel e as in 'bed'. Enlarging your smile makes for a brighter sounding e. The smile lifts the soft palate, enlarging your resonator.

problem as singing with too small a mouth opening. Likewise, opening your mouth vertically yields a different tone than opening it horizontally, as if you smile.

Purse

Classical singers often lightly purse their lips on certain vowels, as if they were a flower. This enhances the projection of your voice, which is essential if you don't use a microphone to make your singing audible and intelligible.

The shape of your resonator

Lip positioning influences how you sound simply because it directly affects the shape of your main resonator — your mouth. Lip positioning is one of the main elements of articulation. Slight lip variations change your sound or timbre a bit.
Larger movements change it so much that you hear a different vowel: After all, going from ah to oh is mainly a matter of repositioning your lips. When you do so very slowly, you'll find that you produce a range of different in-between timbres or sounds as you do.

YOUR TONGUE

Your tongue also plays an important part in the sound you produce. The main thing to do with this flexible organ, though, is not to think too much about it. Focusing on what you should and shouldn't do with your tongue often results in a rigid tongue — and that doesn't help your singing at all.

Relaxed

Your tongue is instrumental in coloring the sound: It changes the shape of the inside of your main resonator. You can use your tongue to produce a wide variety of vowels (slide from ah to ee, for example), consonants, and other sounds. When tongue activity is not required, it's best when you leave it relaxed, its tip loosely resting against the inside of your bottom teeth.

Retracted tongue

Your tongue only needs extra attention if it hinders your singing in any way. Some singers tend to retract their tongue, especially when singing their lowest notes. This constricts the sound. Others use the base of their tongue to force the larynx down, which is not the way you should do it. Singing high notes often seems to create tension in the tongue too.

Convex, concave, grooved, and trembling tongues

Keeping your tongue in a convex or a concave position isn't helpful for your singing either, and neither is — subconsciously — creating a lengthwise groove in it. Why? Because all of this means tension, and tension impedes singing. Another thing to avoid is the high-tension tongue tremolo, in which the tongue trembles when singing a vibrato.

THE VOICE BOX

The voice box or larynx is where your voice is generated. It houses the vocal folds, and includes the cartilages and the muscles that control them. Besides the many different ways the parts of the voice box can move, the entire box can move up and down too.

> ***In detail***
>
> *Most of the movements of the various parts of the larynx (vocal folds, cricoid, thyroid, arytenoids, and others) are not under conscious control. They're also extremely complex. There are plenty of books that describe this part of the vocal instrument in detail.*

Up and down

When singers and teachers talk about controlling the larynx, they usually mean controlling its height. If you're an untrained singer, your voice box tends to go up and down automatically. It will probably move up a little when you start singing, and a little more as you sing higher notes. When dropping in pitch, the voice box moves down again. You can easily see this with male adult singers: Look at their Adam's apple. Female singers and boys can *feel* their voice box moving up and down; simply put your hand on the throat.

Up or down

Singing well has a lot to do with controlling these up-and-down movements. The best position of the voice box depends on the style of music you sing, or the way you sing.

Down

Classical singers usually keep their larynx in a low position. This expands the vocal tract. Just like a guitar with a bigger soundbox, a larger vocal tract makes for a warmer, rounder, darker, 'classical' timbre. Gently pursed lips enhance this sound. Lowering the larynx is also said to increase the resonant capacity of the voice, especially as it's often combined with raising the soft palate.

Up

Conversely, a high larynx reduces the size of your vocal tract. Like a guitar with a smaller body, this makes for a brighter, more focused sound. Many pop, rock, and musical theatre singers let their voice box rise (rather than forcing it upward!) when singing high notes. Doing so without any unnecessary strain and muscle tension may require the help of a teacher.

Peking Opera

Another and very different style of high-larynx singing is employed by vocalists in the traditional Peking Opera and the Japanese Kabuki Theatre, with their very bright, shrill voices.

In-between

Other schools of singing promote a relaxed, stabilized, natural larynx position, similar to where it is when you speak (*e.g.*, speech level singing or speech quality singing).

Covering

Lowering the voice box to make vowels sound warmer or

rounder, and to soften the brittle edge of a bright timbre, is generally known as covering. As it slightly modifies the sound of your vowels, it is also referred to as *vowel mutation* or *vowel modification.*

Larger range, easier transition

Covering not only darkens the vowels. It also helps to avoid breaks between registers, mainly in the male voice, and it allows men to extend the range of their heavy register: They can sing higher notes without switching to their light register.

Classical and non-classical

Traditionally, covering is considered a classical technique. Many non-classical singers avoid it, to not sound too classical. Some non-classical schools of singing, however, promote this technique too.

OVERTONES

Why do certain vowels, pitches, or timbres make your cheeks vibrate, or your skull, your chest bone, or that small spot under your chin? How can operatic singers sing over an orchestra without a microphone? Why is it impossible to hear the difference between the vowels in the highest range of the female voice? To answer these and many other questions that are covered in the following sections, you'll need to know a bit about sound and overtones.

Vibrating air

Simply put, sound is vibrating air. The faster it vibrates, the higher the pitch of the sound will be. Stretch a rubber band, make it vibrate, and listen to the sound. Now stretch it a bit further. You'll see that it starts vibrating faster, and you'll hear a higher pitch.

A guitar string

If you look closely, you'll see that the rubber band seems to vibrate at different frequencies as you change the tension — and it does indeed. Just like a guitar string, for example. When you play the low A-string of a guitar, it vibrates 110 times per second (110 hertz, or 110Hz).

The table of 110

But that's not all! At the same time, each half of that string also vibrates at twice that speed (220Hz). And each third piece of the string vibrates three times as fast (330Hz) — and so on, up to frequencies of 20,000Hz and higher.

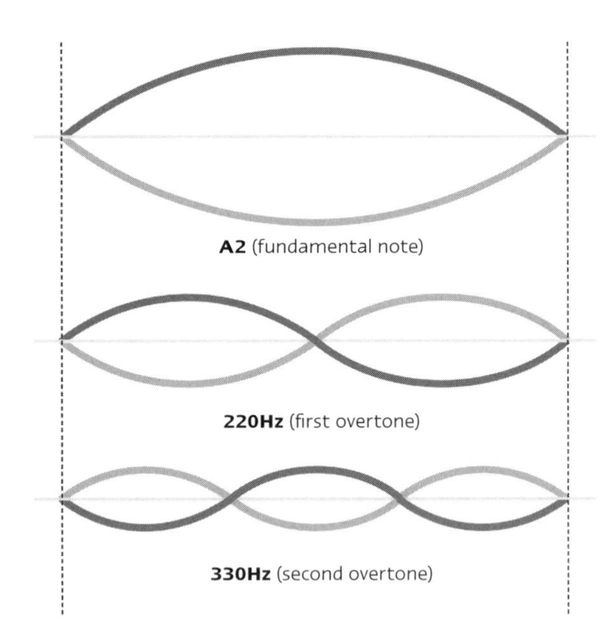

A guitar string vibrates at various speeds: the fundamental pitch and a number of overtones.

Overtones

These 'additional' frequencies are known as *overtones*, *harmonics*, or *partials*. Every instrument produces these overtones, and that includes the human voice.

Guitar or cello?

If a cellist plays the same A note as the guitar player, the string produces the same overtones as the guitar string (220Hz, 330Hz, etc.). You can tell that it's not a guitar, though.

Different intensities

How come? Because the overtones of the cello have different intensities. One instrument might stress the even overtones, for example, and another stresses the uneven overtones. If this sounds too simple, just imagine how many combinations you can make with 20,000-plus different frequencies at different volume levels!

Another resonator

You can tell a saxophone from a clarinet because their resonators have different shapes. These differently shaped resonators create different overtone intensities, and thus recognizably different timbres.

Changing the resonator

Back to the human voice: You can tell an *a* from an *o* because of the same reason — a differently shaped resonator. Basically, the different vowels and many other sounds you produce are all a matter of producing different overtone intensities, and you do so by using your articulators to change the shape of your main resonator — your mouth.

A recognizable mix

In other words: Each vowel produces a recognizable mix of stronger and weaker overtones. You can tell one vowel from the other just like you can tell a sax from a clarinet, or a violin from a banjo.

Too high

When a female opera singer sings her highest notes, it's impossible to distinguish her vowels. Why? These highest notes produce so few effective overtones that the differences between the vowels fade.

Bright or subdued

You can make your vowels sound bright or subdued — apart from those very high ones, maybe — in the same way that you produce different vowels: by varying the position of your tongue or your lips, thus changing the shape of your resonator. As a result, certain overtones will be stressed or reduced.

Treble control

Stressing higher overtones (*i.e.*, higher frequencies) will make for a brighter timbre; reducing them will produce a darker, warmer sound. This is very similar to turning the treble control of an amp up or down.

Resonating objects

If you play a CD, especially at higher volumes, certain objects in the room may start vibrating along with the music at certain frequencies.

Likewise, various parts of your body can vibrate sympathetically along with your voice. If you sing a vowel at a certain pitch or with a certain timbre, you can produce and enhance (overtone) frequencies that may cause your skull, your chest bone, or any other parts of your body to vibrate along — or any object in the room you're in.

Stop

These sympathetic vibrations result from the sound you produce. If you stop your skull or chest bone from vibrating (by simply holding them) you won't sound different. This may be hard to believe, as it will most probably *feel* different to you. You may also *hear* it differently — but your audience won't.

RESONANCE AND TIMBRE

Resonance and timbre are closely related subjects. In just a few words: You can produce different timbres (and vowels, and other sounds) by influencing the resonances in your vocal tract. You do so by positioning your active articulators: your tongue, lower jaw, lips, and soft palate. Again, this reduces or boosts certain overtones.

Articulation

Of course, you also use your articulators for proper *articulation*: the exact way you shape your vowels and consonants. Articulation is dealt with on pages 74–78.

Your personal timbre

Every human being has a personal, recognizable timbre, as unique as their fingerprints. Your personal sound or timbre is mostly determined by the specific dimensions of your vocal tract and other parts of your vocal instrument.

An example

For example, a wide, flattish palate is said to promote a darker sounding voice. A high, narrow palate would result in a lighter timbre. In other words: Differently shaped palates produce overtones in different intensities, which makes for recognizably different timbres. The same goes for many other elements of the human voice. Generally speaking, a larger vocal tract will make for a darker sound; a smaller vocal tract will promote a brighter timbre — just like a baritone saxophone has a darker timbre compared to the much smaller soprano saxophone.

Type of voice

Your personal timbre is a major element in determining your type of voice. A tenor's range is higher than that of a baritone, and his timbre is much lighter. An alto may have a range that's very close to that of a soprano, but the alto has a warmer, darker timbre.

Your style

Your timbre can also be a decisive factor in determining which styles of music you can sing with more or less success, and which styles of music you'd better not sing if you don't want to damage your vocal instrument.

Emotions

So some things are fixed, when it comes to timbre. But within those limits, you can do a lot to vary the timbre or color of your voice. You can make your voice sound happy, angry, heavy or light, and so on — and you don't need a teacher for that purpose. When you feel sad, nobody needs to tell you how to sound sad. The timbre often comes along automatically with the emotion.

Improving your tone

You may be able to improve your control over your timbre. Singing is very much like playing a musical instrument. Learning how to make an instrument sound doesn't require substantial practice, but making it sound good takes years. Likewise, almost everybody can sing, but improving and learning to control your tone — to make your singing voice sound the way you want it to — can take many years.

Non-classical singers

This doesn't go for classical singers only. As a non-classical singer you can learn how to make better use of your specific timbre, or how to overcome problems, how to stress the strong points and reduce the lesser qualities of your voice, how to produce the timbre you want without hurting your vocal instrument, and so on, without losing your trademark sound, your authenticity, or anything else.

Sax players and guitarists

On most musical instruments, it's not that hard to give a student basic instructions on how to improve or adjust the tone. You can tell a violinist not to press the bow too hard; you can tell a sax player to not put the mouthpiece too far in his mouth; you can tell a guitarist to produce a brighter tone by playing closer to the bridge.

Invisible

For singers, this doesn't work, as most elements of the vocal instrument are invisible, and many of these elements are not under conscious control. It is no use telling a singer to lift his arytenoids a bit, or to relax his *conus elasticus*...

Some examples

This is one of the reasons that singers and teachers talk about various types of resonance, for example, or about 'singing in the mask': They talk about what they want you to hear or feel, rather than about what you should do to get there. Here are some examples, used in a variety of schools of singing.

Resonance

The different sounds, pitches, and timbres you produce can generate vibrations in various parts of your body. These are often referred to as *chest resonance* and *head resonance*, for example.

Chest and head

Singing a note with 'chest resonance' typically means singing it in a way that you can feel your chest vibrating along with the note you sing. This produces a darker timbre than singing the same note with head resonance. Using 'head resonance' results in a brighter, more brilliant timbre that has a ring or a twang to it.

Pitch and resonance

Chest resonance, head resonance, throat resonance, mouth resonance, and other types of resonance are sometimes associated with pitches or pitch ranges: Low notes are said to have chest resonance, notes in the middle range are said to have *throat resonance*, and high notes have head resonance, for example.

Register

Of course, there's a link here with the way many singers name the various registers of the singing voice: the *chest register* for the lowest part of the range, and the *head register* for the highest part of the range, for example. Each register has its own timbre. Chapter 5 deals extensively with this subject.

Timbre and resonance

Other schools of thought don't link types of resonance to specific pitch ranges or registers. They speak of using head resonance or *head voice* to add brightness to low notes, for instance. This would be a way to create an even timbre throughout your range: High notes sound less shrill with some extra 'chest' warmth or darkness, and low notes sound more musical if they have some brightness to them.

Not everyone

Not everyone agrees. Even within one style of singing, there are many different opinions. Here are four views on one subject: Some classical singers say you should never use chest resonance or *chest voice*; others say you should never use pure chest resonance, but always create a blend. Some say you should never use chest resonance in your high range, yet others say they always do, even on their very highest notes...

Mmm

You can easily feel what the various types of resonances are referring to. Hum an *mmm* at a comfortable pitch. Maintain the pitch, and try to send the sound to various places in your body. When you do, you'll find that you — if even ever so slightly — change the shape of your vocal tract, maybe by changing the position of your larynx, by lowering or lifting your soft palate, by repositioning your lips. Thus, you generate different overtone intensities. The stronger, accentuated overtones you produce can make different parts of your body vibrate sympathetically.

The right words

Do the vibrations or 'resonances' in your chest or head actually contribute to the sound you produce? Some say they do — others point out that your head and your chest cannot actually resonate, as they're filled with non-resonating substances: your brain and your lungs, respectively. Filling a resonator (*e.g.*, the soundbox of a violin or a guitar) with similar substances would simply kill all of its resonating capacities. Who's right, however, is not the issue of this book.

The main thing is that your teacher or the author of the book you read uses words and images that help you understand and improve your voice.

The right timbre

It's also important to know that the vibrations you feel often differ from the vibrations another singer feels — just like different glasses vibrate along to different tones and overtones. The main thing, when it comes to singing, is that the vibrations you feel can help you reproduce a certain timbre. If you know that this one note sounded great when you felt vibrations in your cheeks, reproducing these vibrations can help you reproduce that timbre.

True or not?

There are many more approaches. Some are quite close to what's actually happening in your body, your larynx, or your head; others tend to deny how it really works. As long as they're effective in getting singers to sing better, you may wonder how bad they are.

The back or the front

For example, some teachers will tell you to visualize using the back of your vocal folds, toward the neck, for low notes and dark timbres (and to produce belly-laughs, or to show a big dog that you're really serious). For high and bright notes (and giggles, and baby talk) it's suggested you focus on the front part of your vocal folds.

Placement

Singers often talk about *placing the voice* in this context. So you can read about 'mentally placing the voice on the front part of your vocal folds.' Placement is also used to indicate where you should or could feel vibrations: 'placing the voice in the nose,' for example.

Focus

'Placing the voice forward' usually refers to what's also known as focus: singing in a way that your voice projects well. One popular image to help you focus your voice is to pretend you're singing through a small hole — yet with a wide open mouth. If you don't focus, your voice will not project.

The mask

Another term you'll come across in many books and methods is the *mask*. The mask is the 'inside of your face,' which refers mainly to the area behind and around your nose. 'Singing into the mask' or placing the voice in the mask is often said to add definition, presence, brightness, power, or projection to your voice.

Classical or non-classical

Though many non-classical singers use the 'mask' as described above, others consider placing the voice into the mask as something only classical singers do. Among classical singers,

Singing into the mask: promoted by some, rejected by others.

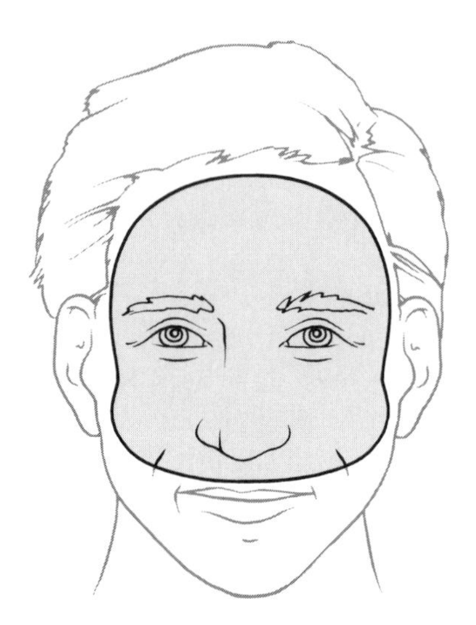

however, opinions on the concept of singing into the mask differ at least as much.

Strain

Other singers — both classical and non-classical — don't use the mask or similar concepts at all: They strongly feel that trying to evoke vibrations or resonances in certain parts of the body (the mask, the chin, the cheeks, or anywhere else) can easily cause unwanted strain. The concept of the mask is also said to hinder the coloration of your voice — *i.e.*, your ability to create various timbres or colors.

The voice box

Likewise, some teachers dislike the concept of placing the voice in certain parts of the head or the body. One of the reasons given is that concentrating too much on where to place the voice tends to distract the singer from the very source of his or her voice: the voice box.

Different ways

A common problem with terms such as 'placement' and 'the mask' is that they're used in many different ways — so always make sure you know what the other person is referring to.

Nasal timbre

For example, singing into the mask is also sometimes linked to singing in languages with a more or less nasal timbre, such as French or Brazilian. Singers often feel these sounds in their nose, or in their 'mask.' What actually happens is that you lower your soft palate, giving access to the nasal cavity: This makes for the nasal timbre that makes French words like *quinze* (fifteen) or mon (my) sound really French. So while singing with a nasal 'congested' timbre is highly undesirable in many languages, it is required that you do so in others.

Tipcode VOCALS-009
Angela demonstrates how 'nasal' the French words mon, jambe, feminin, timbre, *and* quinze *can sound.*

Guttural timbre

The same goes for a guttural timbre. In Western classical music and many styles of non-classical music, singing 'from the throat' is considered a bad habit. However, many schools of performance, such as the traditional female choirs from Bulgaria, are famous for their harsh, almost brassy, guttural timbre. What singing well means differs per style of music, per culture, per era, and so on — and what's considered a beautiful timbre depends on at least as many factors.

Helpful sensations

As a singer, you don't hear yourself the way your audience does. Most of what you hear comes from within, through bone conduction and through your *Eustachian tubes* (the tubes that connect your ears with your oral cavity). As you can't properly judge your timbre that way, the vibrations and other sensations you can feel in your body can be very helpful in reproducing a certain timbre.

Hand behind your ear

To increase the amount of sound that reaches your outer ears, simply cup your hands behind them — though this will help just a bit. If you really want to find out how your voice sounds to others, you'll have to record it. These recordings will provide valuable feedback, but they won't help you to control or adjust your timbre as you sing.

Inner ear

You can improve your control over your timbre by training your 'inner ear.' When you really get to know your voice, the sound you hear from within can tell you whether you sound good, or whether you need to make adjustments, and so on.

Plugging your ears

Some teachers even advise that you practice using your inner ear by singing with your ears plugged. This helps to get you familiar with your voice as you hear it from the inside, so you can rely on that information in certain situations.

Bad monitoring

Holding one or both ears can also be helpful when you're singing amplified and you can't hear yourself due to bad or insufficient monitoring.

FORMANTS AND THE SINGER'S FORMANT

The fact that opera singers can sing over a hundred-piece orchestra has nothing to do with volume. It's all a matter of resonance. And so is creating a perfect, classical timbre.

Classical and non-classical
The following section is mainly of interest to classical singers, but subheadings identify areas of interest to non-classical singers too.

Singing strings
If you have a piano at hand, open the lid, press the right pedal down, and sing an *ah* into the piano. If you listen carefully, you'll hear that the strings will sound an *ah*. Now sing an *e*, an *o*, or any other vowel. The strings will duplicate your vowels almost perfectly.

Very similar
How this works is pretty straightforward: Each vowel is formed by certain overtones or frequencies.
When you sing a vowel into an open piano, its frequencies trigger the corresponding frequencies of the strings. The strings, in turn, produce a very similar sound.

Formants
In the mouth and throat cavity, the main resonators of your voice, there are five areas of resonance that are crucial in forming the vowels. These *formants* or *formant areas* amplify the specific frequencies for each vowel.

Speak or sing
When you speak or sing, you change the shape of your resonator to form vowels, consonants, and other sounds, and you activate the relevant formants unconsciously.

Formant tuning
Classical singers go one important step further. They are trained to make full use of the formants by matching them to the overtones of the fundamental notes they're singing. This is known as *formant tuning*.

Free amplification
If you're capable of making this match, the formants offer 'free amplification' of your voice. They add clarity and brightness to your sound and make it project.

Adapt your vowels

Formant tuning often requires you to change the (overtone) frequencies of your vowels in order to make the match with the formants. You do so by adapting your pronunciation, for example by making a wide *ah* a bit less wide, or by making an *ee* a bit brighter.

Singer's formant

The fact that opera singers can sing over a hundred-piece orchestra has a lot to do with the free amplification that formants offer: Opera singers cluster the third, fourth and fifth formants to produce a very strong, ringing frequency known as the *singer's formant* or the *ring of the voice*. It is that frequency that helps them project over an orchestra: not volume, but overtones with a very strong resonance. The frequency of the singer's formant is usually said to be around 2,400–3,000Hz.

Practice

Can you develop or train the singer's formant? Some experts say anybody can; others say you can only develop it if you happen to 'have' it, referring to certain physical aspects (*e.g.*, a specific shape of the *epiglottis*).

Men and women?

Some experts say that only men have a singer's formant, and that female classical singers use formant tuning to the same effect. Others say that women do have a singer's formant, but only in their lower range, up to E5. At higher pitches, the human voice doesn't produce enough overtones to create a singer's formant.

Non-classical singers?

Can non-classical singers use the singer's formant too? Some say they could, but the resulting timbre would be undeniably classical. Others say every good singer has this quality to a certain extent, and yet others say non-classical singers just don't.

Non-classical singers

The main thing, in this context, is that the frequency range of the singer's formant is obviously crucial to the human voice. That goes for non-classical singing too: Many vocal microphones have a higher sensitivity in this range, giving your voice an extra boost. And if you have a hard time hearing yourself through your monitor speakers, don't ask the sound engineer to turn the volume up, but to boost the 2,400–3,000Hz range a little instead!

More about formants

There's a lot more to say about formants and the singer's formant, but most goes beyond the framework of this book. It may be nice to know, though, that the first formant (F1) helps amplify overtones in the frequency range up to a 1,000Hz. You can adapt its exact frequency by moving your jaw up and down (according to some experts), or by lowering or raising your larynx (according to other experts), or both (a third group of experts…). The frequency range for the second formant (F2), which is said to respond to the position and shape of your tongue, is 1,000–2,000Hz. These first two are the main formants for the pronunciation of vowels. The other three formants cover higher frequency ranges.

Formants, timbre, placement

If you compare the two preceding sections (Resonance, page 54; Formants, page 62), you may find that they both deal with the same subject. Formant tuning, after all, involves adjusting your articulators so that certain frequencies can match and amplify each other. Adjusting your articulators changes the shape of your resonator. This influences overtone intensities, and thus resonances, and therefore your timbre, possibly producing vibrations or other sensations in your body or your head, which by some is seen as placing your voice in a different way.

VOLUME

The human voice can sound extremely loud, but you can sing or speak very softly as well. In other words: The vocal instrument has a very large *dynamic range*. Larger than many musical instruments, in fact.

Not volume...

Well-trained singers and singers with very powerful voices can easily produce as much sound as a piano, or even a drum set. However, singers hardly ever rely just on sheer volume to make themselves audible.

... but projection or amplification

Classical singers learn to project their voices, and projection has to do with resonance, not volume (see page 63). Non-classical singers simply use a microphone and have their voices amplified, so even the smallest voice can fill a stadium.

Big or small

Some people can generate more sound than others. That doesn't make them better singers; they just have bigger voices. The 'size' of your voice isn't that important, though it can limit the number of styles of music you can be successful in. Some types of music require big voices and may be detrimental for small voices, for example, but there are many songs that sound better with a small voice.

Dynamics

You can improve your singing by extending your control over your dynamic range. This means that you learn to make full use of your maximum volume, so you can sing as loud as you can without hurting your voice, or really softly without sounding breathy or losing your voice.

Belting

One well-known technique that allows you to sing loudly, high notes without hurting your voice is known as belting. *There's more on this technique on pages 95–96, and in Chapter 7.*

Breath support

Breath support (see page 42) is essential for singing both loudly and softly. You need to generate a powerful air stream to sing loudly, and you need breath support so as not to spill it all in one word. If you sing softly, you need breath support to prevent your air supply from flowing out without pinching your throat.

Volume and timbre

Most wind instruments sound smooth and warm when played softly. Playing louder makes the sound fuller and bigger; if played even louder it can get harsh and eventually break up. Your voice, which functions essentially as a wind instrument, tends to do the same.

Louder – but don't scream

Learning to sing well includes learning to control your timbre over your entire dynamic range. Of course, your timbre changes as you start to sing louder, but it shouldn't sound like someone else is taking over, nor should it sound like you're screaming. Likewise, your voice should stay clear and full as you start to sing softer, and it shouldn't turn into a whisper right away.

Volume and pitch

Learning to sing well is also about matching volume and pitch.

Messa di voce

There's a famous exercise for developing control over volume and timbre, known as messa di voce. Pitch control and breath support also benefit from this exercise. In basic terms, messa di voce involves breathing in once and singing a single vowel in that same breath, starting very softly, gradually growing louder, and then back, maintaining the desired timbre and the original pitch. Despite its classical Italian name, this is a great exercise for non-classical singers too. Being able to sing any note in your range at various volumes makes you a more expressive vocalist.

Many singers tend to get louder as they sing higher notes, and vice versa: Your lowest notes do not allow for much volume. Just sing your lowest note and try to make it sound loud, and you'll see what happens.

Tipcode VOCALS-011
This is what messa di voce sounds like: Singing a single vowel, starting very softly, gradually growing louder, and back.

IN TUNE

If you have trouble singing in tune, the information on the next few pages may offer you some helpful hints. If you don't, you may skip this section: Being too conscious of what singing in tune is all about can easily make you sing out of tune…

Afraid

Most people who say they can't sing, say so because they're afraid to sing out of tune. And when you are afraid, you probably *will* sing out of tune.

Tone deaf?

People who really have trouble singing in tune are often considered to be *tone deaf.* Strictly speaking, however, there's no such thing as tone deafness. First of all, 'tone deaf' people are often perfectly able to tell a wrong note from a right note. Secondly, as you can only recognize vowels because of their specific overtones, 'tone deaf' people wouldn't be able to hear what you say either — but they do. So as some experts say, tone deafness doesn't exist, but anxiety to sing in tune certainly does. Learning to sing in tune can be mainly a matter of reducing anxiety.

Other things

To learn to sing in tune, it is important to learn to focus on things other than hitting the right note. Teachers have access to a wide variety of exercises and techniques to help you sing in tune. *Ear training* is a key subject, teaching you to hear and feel pitches and pitch differences. Breath support is equally important, as it allows you to maintain a certain pitch. Also, you may have to learn to imagine the note in your head before you actually sing it.

Flat, sharp, can't hit, can't sustain...

Some people always sing too low (*flat*); others sing too high (*sharp*). Some aspiring singers can't hit a certain pitch; others can hit it, but don't succeed in sustaining it. You can sing out of tune because you're untrained; because you have a hearing deficiency or a lack of breath support, or because you are unfocused or hungry, or because you're singing notes that don't fit your range... What can make singing in tune so hard, and what can you do to make it easier?

By yourself

Singing in tune is quite hard if you sing by yourself, without the accompaniment of an instrument that you can relate your notes to. If you sing without any accompaniment, you can only relate your next note to the one you're singing.

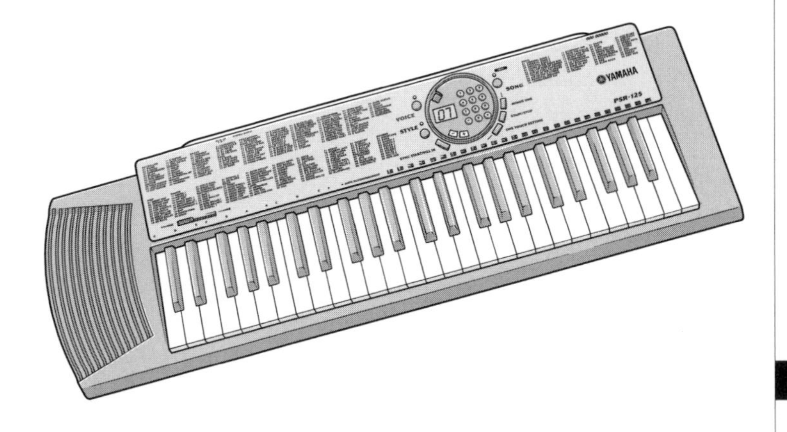

Even a low-budget keyboard can be of great help.

Keyboard or CD

That's why using a keyboard, a guitar, or another instrument can be very helpful in your vocal practice: It helps you hit and sustain your notes. Alternatively, you can practice using CDs, tapes, or other media with prerecorded exercises.

In a choir

Singing in tune is probably easiest in a choir: It's often quite easy to 'copy' the pitch that the people around you are singing. Besides, if the choir is big enough, and your voice is small enough, you may even sing a bit out of tune without anyone noticing.

Accepted

Some experts insist that the vocal instrument is almost incapable of sounding perfectly in tune. That's nothing to worry about, though. For some reason, minor pitch deviations of the singing voice are much more acceptable than out-of-tune pianos, guitars, or other instruments. The singer's 'automatic' vibrato probably has something to do with this (see page 80).

Too low, too high

In non-classical music, there are quite a lot of famous vocalists who hardly ever sing in tune. Many popular singers in rock, pop, jazz, Latin, and other styles seem to sing just a bit too low, often with a somewhat husky, subdued timbre. Others tend to sing a tad sharp all the time. These deviations wouldn't be accepted in classical singing, but they are in most non-classical styles. In part, this is because the performance, the lyrics, and the emotions of the vocalist tend to overshadow the importance of singing in perfect pitch. Singing consistently flat or sharp can even be a personal and musically appealing trademark.

Perfect

If you realize that you have to tune your voice for every single note you sing, it's almost a miracle that people can sing in tune at all. A split second before you sing a note, your multi-muscle-operated vocal folds have to adjust to the tension that's required for the exact pitch you're after. This adjustment is known as *prephonatory tuning*. To make this work, you do of course need to 'know' the pitch you want to produce, and your vocal folds have to adjust accordingly.

Bending up or down

Without prephonatory tuning, you would have to correct each note as you sing it. Untrained singers sometimes sing that way: They just start singing a note at a certain pitch, and bend it up or down until it sounds right to them (which is no guarantee that it really is).

Fall-off

Bending the pitch isn't always a sign of bad singing, though. In various styles, singers consciously use pitch bends as an effect, either bending the note up or down to the intended pitch, or way down at the end of a phrase (known as a *fall-off*). Wind instrument players, guitarists, and other instrumentalists use similar ornamentations.

Tipcode VOCALS-012

In this Tipcode, Angela demonstrates how you can bend pitches up or down.

Ear training

To be able to hit a note at the right pitch, you need to know what that pitch is. If this is difficult, ear training and other exercises may be of help. Note that some singers tend to sing higher notes too high, and lower notes too low; others hardly seem to know where to find the next note at all. There are several do-it-yourself ear-training programs available (CDs, cassettes, software,

Internet), but only a good teacher can help to pick the exercises that are designed to solve your specific problem.

Concentration

Singing in tune also demands focus and concentration: After all, you need to 'tune' your instrument for every single note.

Too much

Strange as it seems, concentrating too much on singing in tune can easily make you sing out of tune. It's a bit like trying not to think of pink elephants: If someone tells you to, you probably can't. Rather than focus on pitch alone, try to work on anticipating the note you're going to sing, and work on other aspects of your vocal technique.

Hit and drop

Other singers have no problem hitting the right pitch at once, but they can't sustain it: The pitch drops or rises as they hold the note. This can usually be solved by improving breath support (see page 42). Lack of focus can also result in unsteady pitch: You have to stay with the tone as you sing it, not just throw it out and let it go.

Areas

There also may be areas in your range where you tend to sing more out of tune than others. Concentrating on these areas and giving them more focus may be all you need to do.

Out of your range

If you have problems singing the highest or lowest notes of a song in tune, you may want to transpose the song, changing its key. Problems hitting the highest notes? Transposing the song to a lower key may solve the problem. Can't reach the lowest notes? Make the entire song higher in pitch by transposing it to a higher key. Likewise, many art songs (*Lieder*) are available in various keys.

Hard or harder

Guitarists and other instrumentalists may not be really happy if you want to change the key of a song. Transposing it can make it harder to play for them — requiring less common fingerings, for example. Having to sing notes at the extremes of your range is usually even harder, though.

Another timbre

Singing a song in another key not only makes a song sound lower or higher. It also changes its timbre a bit: Every key has its own character.

Food

Some singers find it harder to sing in tune too long or too soon after having enjoyed a meal. Eating right before or too long before a performance can affect your singing in other ways too (see pages 115 and 127).

Headphones

To be able to sing in tune, you need to be able to hear yourself properly. That explains why it's impossible to sing along to a CD that you listen to through a pair of headphones. Likewise, if you sing using any kind of amplification, it is crucial that you can hear yourself. If you don't, you'll have problems. There's one trick that can temporarily solve the problem: If you close one or both ears, you can hear your voice from inside, even if there is a lot of noise around you.

Monitor speakers

In order to hear yourself, you'll need one or more proper monitor speakers. Turning their volume up may not be the best solution if you can't hear your voice. If you hear yourself too loudly, chances are that you'll still sing out of tune.

Turn it up

Instead, you can ask the sound engineer to turn up the 800–1,400Hz or 3,000Hz range a bit (see page 65). Lowering the volume level of the other instruments or monitors you're hearing can help too.

Pitch correction

To help out singers who can't sing in tune at all, or to correct the odd out-of-tune note for singers who can, there's equipment that can actually make pitch corrections in real time, as you sing (see page 162)! Correcting pitch in a recording is even less of a problem. Most audio editing software can do that for you.

ARTICULATION

Articulation a confusing term. In the following section, it is used for the way you 'shape' and link individual letters. You do so using your active articulators: lips, lower jaw, tongue, and soft palate.

Timbre

The term articulation is also used to refer to timbre, as described on page 54. After all, both timbre and vowels are the sonic result of the overtones you produce by using your articulators.

Pronunciation

You can articulate very well even with a terrible pronunciation. In this book, the term 'pronunciation' is reserved for making words sound the way they should in the language or dialect you're singing in, as discussed in Chapter 9, *Lyrics.*

Diction

Sometimes, the word *diction* is used to indicate the combined result of articulation (how you shape and combine letters in speech or music) and pronunciation (how your words sound).

Inarticulate

If you don't articulate well, if you sing 'under your breath' or 'between your teeth,' you'll have a hard time getting your lyrics across. You'll sound indistinct and, yes, *inarticulate.*

Tension

Sometimes, singers tend to use a lot of tension to articulate well, and tension doesn't help your singing. Articulation exercises are designed to help you speak and sing clearly and understandably, using a minimum amount of tension.

The basics

To understand the basics of articulation, it's good to know a bit more about vowels and consonants, and about how you produce them.

Vowels

The alphabet has just a few vowels, but there are many ways to pronounce them, each one requiring a different articulation. Just listen to the *a* in the words *lame*, *mall*, *rather*, *damage*, and *any*. In other languages there are even more ways to articulate the letter *a*, like the wide open first sound of the French word *amour* (love) or the German word *Aria*.

Different vowels, same sound

The reverse is quite common too: There are some differently written vowels and vowel combinations that require an identical articulation. Just listen to the *e* sound in the following words *he* [e], *believe* [ie], *tea* [ea], *key* [ey], and *machine* [i] and notice their very different spellings.

Tongue and lips

Articulating all the various vowel sounds is mainly a matter of raising different areas of your tongue and assuming various lip positions. For example, to articulate the *i* as in *meet*, you bring the front part of your tongue close to the palate. For the *u* as in *moon*, you raise the back part. The *e* in *bed* is articulated raising the middle of your tongue, and when you articulate the *a* in *rather* your tongue is low.

Diagrams

There are complete diagrams of the various tongue positions. You can find them in more technical books on singing and on the Internet.

Diphthongs

In some syllables, you need to glide from one vowel sound to the next. The word glide demonstrates this perfectly. This is known as a *diphthong*. Diphthongs are also heard in words like hour and toy.

Triphthongs

A *triphthong* is a combination of three vowel sounds in one syllable, and sometimes even in one single character: the *i* in tire. A low tongue at first, raising it in the middle of the syllable, and moving it toward the back when approaching the R.

Consonants

Vowels require an uninterrupted, open air flow. Most consonants require you to interrupt the air flow (*e.g.*, P), or to restrict it (*e.g.*, S). You can do so in various ways and at various places in your vocal tract; that's what makes for the variety of sounds. Different categories have been created to catalog the various types of consonants; the listings below are not intended to be complete.

Lips, teeth, velum, glottis

One group of categories indicates where you interrupt or reduce the air flow.

- *Bilabials* ('two lips') are consonants that require closing your lips (M), or closing and opening them: B, P.
- *Labiodentals* are made using a lip and your teeth: F, V.
- *Alveolars* require you to stop or reduce the air stream with your tongue against the sockets of your teeth (your alveoli): Z, T, S, D. Alveolars are also known as *linguadentals*; *lingua* is Latin for tongue.
- *Interdentals* are articulated using your tongue as well as your upper and lower teeth (*th*ough).
- *Velar consonants* require you to lower and then raise your velum or soft palate: *g*o, *c*an.
- *Glottal consonants* use the opening between the vocal folds (the glottis): H.

Plosives, glides, and nasals

Other categories refer to the way the consonant is articulated.

- *Plosives* or *stop-plosives* are articulated as small explosions: You build up air pressure and then let it go, by opening your lips (bilabials: B, P), by taking your tongue off of your teeth (alveolars: D, T), or by raising your velum and lowering the back of your tongue (*g*o).
- *Fricatives* are articulated by letting air out through a very small opening, creating a lot of *friction* or turbulence. You can do this with your lips and teeth (labiodentals), with your tongue against the sockets of your teeth (alveolars), or with your vocal folds.
- An *affricative* is a plosive followed by a fricative (*ch*allenge, *j*udge).
- *Nasals* use your nose. Blocking your nose stops the sound. The 'ng' sound in the word si*ng*ing is a good example.
- *Laterals* are produced by letting air pass by on one or both (lateral) sides of the tongue: L.
- The L is also categorized as a *liquid consonant*, just like the R. They're produced by a rather delicate contact between tongue and mouth.
- *Glides* just glide, like wind.

Voiced and voiceless

You can also distinguish between consonants that use the vocal folds (*voiced consonants*: B, D, G, J, L, M, N, R, V, Z) and the ones that don't (*voiceless consonants*: P, F, S, T).

The main difference

With some pairs of consonants, the usage of the vocal folds is the main difference: the voiced V and the voiceless F; the voiced Z and the voiceless S, and so on.

Many more

There are many more categories and differentiations that break down the numerous different consonant and vowel sounds humans can produce, in English and in hundreds of other languages.

Impossible

Many of the sounds produced in other languages are very hard if not impossible to articulate for American (and many other) singers. This is because of the way you're trained to use your articulators, as well as what you're used to hearing.
If your language doesn't contain a certain sound, you're likely to be unable to pronounce it simply because you don't recognize it — and not because you have a different vocal instrument. See the section on pronunciation in Chapter 9 for more information.

ONSET OR ATTACK

The *onset* or *attack* refers to the way you initiate vowels and other sounds. Most classical singers seem to use the word onset, while non-classical singers say attack. The ending of a tone, a word, or another sound is known as the *release.*

A plosive a

When people say the word 'absolutely,' for example, you'll often hear a short click sound at the very beginning of the first letter of that word. This is very much like a plosive, yet one that's created with the vocal folds.

Glottal attack

What happens is the following: To articulate a word that begins with a vowel, most people tend to close the opening between the vocal folds (the glottis) rather firmly. Then they build up pressure from the lungs until the vocal folds separate with an explosive click. This is known as *glottal attack* or *glottal initiation.*

Like coughing

In most styles of singing the glottal attack is not appreciated. In recording situations, the explosive clicks can be a real hassle. The glottal attack is often said to be potentially harmful for your vocal health, as forcefully driving the vocal folds apart can result in various symptoms. It's actually just like coughing, which can be considered an extreme form of glottal attack (see page 118). On the other hand, the glottal attack or *coup de glotte* is an essential element in accenting words in German *Lied* (art song) singing, for example.

Breathy attack

To avoid the glottal attack, you can add an almost soundless *h* at the beginning of the word: '*h*'absolutely. Such an *aspirated onset* or *breathy attack* can produce an all-over breathy timbre, however.

Clean attack

The third way to initiate a vowel is usually considered the best: It's the *clean attack* or *simultaneous attack*, which requires the air flow to arrive at the vocal folds at the very moment you close your glottis. This prevents clicks and breathiness.

Two more names

The clean attack or clean onset is also known as *coordinated attack*: It demands coordination of your air flow and your vocal folds. Yet another term is diaphragmatic attack: It involves control of your diaphragm — breath support, in other words. The fifth term is sung attack: You can only do it when you sing.

Release

Similar things happen at the end of a word, a tone, or a sound. You can slam your vocal folds shut (*stopped release* or *glottal stop*),

Grunt

Pronouncing a vowel with a guttural grunt or bite is known as a scraped attack. This can be excruciating for your vocal folds. However, when well placed, it may sound quite nice as an effect.

which may at one point damage them. You can also end a word and stop the sound but continue to let air escape (*breathy release*). The best way to end a word, according to many, is the *clean release.* You stop the sound by opening your glottis, and you control your diaphragm to prevent more air from rushing out.

VIBRATO

When you sing a long note, your tone is probably not straight; the pitch goes up and down a bit all the time. This is known as *vibrato*: slight pitch fluctuations that are usually said to make for a richer, warmer, and more colorful sound. Your vibrato is often considered a very important aspect of your personal timbre too.

Natural

When you sing, your larynx or voice box lightly dances up and down on your air stream. This is what's commonly thought to produce the vibrato. Singing with a straight, steady tone, without vibrato, requires effort and training, as you learn to keep your larynx still. Singing with vibrato comes naturally, in most cases.

Many ways

If you listen to a number of singing styles from different eras and cultures, you'll find that there are many ways to use vibrato, or to avoid it.

Most singers

In classical music, the standards for a 'good vibrato' are much tighter than in most other Western styles of singing — but learning to control your vibrato is something most singers, in any style, can benefit from.

Your voice box

Controlling the vibrato seems to be mainly a matter of controlling the subtle vertical movements of the voice box. If it moves up and down too wildly, you won't be able to produce a steady tone at all.

Good vibrato

A good vibrato is usually said to have around six or seven pitch fluctuations per second (6–7 Hz). At that speed, your vocal muscles seem to have an easy, comfortable balance without any unnecessary tension. The pitch should go up and down about a quarter to maybe a third of a step.

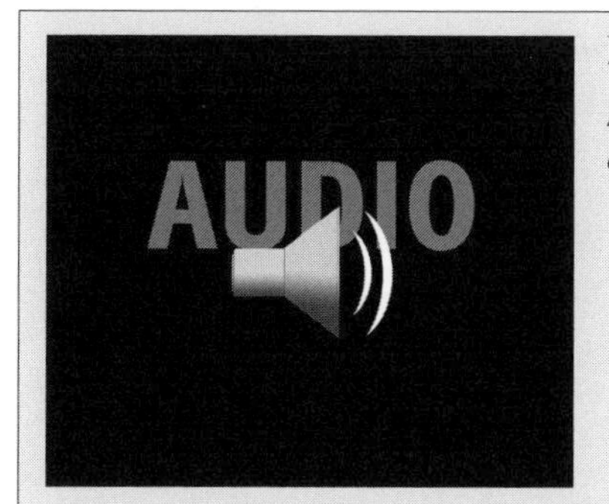

Tipcode VOCALS-013

A brief demonstration of a classical vibrato.

Too slow

A vibrato that fluctuates too slowly often tends to deviate from the original pitch too much. This out-of-tune effect is referred to as a *wobble.*

Too fast

A vibrato that's too fast, fluctuating at more then seven or eight Hertz, doesn't sound like a vibrato anymore. Vocalists usually call this a tremolo. (Instrumentalists use that term to indicate the fast repetition of a single note.)

Louder, softer

The term tremolo is also used to indicate a rhythmic fluctuation in volume level, getting slightly softer and louder as you sing. To make things even more confusing, others (incorrectly) call this effect vibrato. Commonly, however, the slight variations in loudness are considered to be part of the 'natural' vibrato, and you're bound to hear both types of fluctuations in many voices, both trained and untrained.

Boring vibrato

A pleasing vibrato usually has different frequencies; a prominent vibrato using the same frequency all the time may soon become boring to the listener. One singer whose vibrato is too prominent can impose a similar effect on an entire choir. In choir singing, the voices have to blend — so the vibratos have to match.

No vibrato

Various musical styles require singing without a vibrato, one example being Eastern European choral singing. European Baroque and Renaissance vocalists are often said to have sung without vibrato too. Non-vibrato singing is also required in various contemporary classical pieces, and a flat, straight tone is sometimes used to accentuate a shallow, unexpressive, or cold-hearted character in an opera, or to lend a specific character to certain lyrics or melodies.

5

Registers

The human voice, like many other musical instruments, has different registers. Some say two, some say more. This chapter introduces you to the main ideas and terms that you'll come across, shedding light on female and male voices, the passaggio and what to do with it, extreme registers, and belting.

The subject of the registers of the singing voice is so confusing because there is no standard terminology. Singers and vocal experts often use the same name for different registers, as well as different names for the same register. The information in this chapter will help you figure out who's talking about what.

Voice or register?

The first formal teachers of singing, in seventeenth-century Italy, believed that people had two voices: one in the head, for high notes; and one in the chest, for the lower part of your range. The terms *head voice* and *chest voice* stem from that era. Though they're misleading, they're still being used interchangeably with *head register* and *chest register.*

Registers

When you sing your highest notes, your vocal folds vibrate differently than when you sing your lowest notes. As mentioned in Chapter 2, these two different modes of vibration are usually considered the two main registers.

Passaggio

The break or passaggio is where your vocal folds switch from one mode to the other. At which note this happens depends on many things, such as the vowel you are singing and how loud you are singing. The passaggio can also be moved up or down a few notes or more. There's more on this below.

Many voices, one passaggio

No matter how different voices are (male or female, bass or soprano, pro or non-singer), the passaggio always occurs in the same area. This is in the area from C4 (Middle C) to F4, in the middle of the piano keyboard.

Chest, heavy, or modal

The register below the passaggio is commonly known as the chest register. Many experts prefer to call it the *modal register* or *heavy*

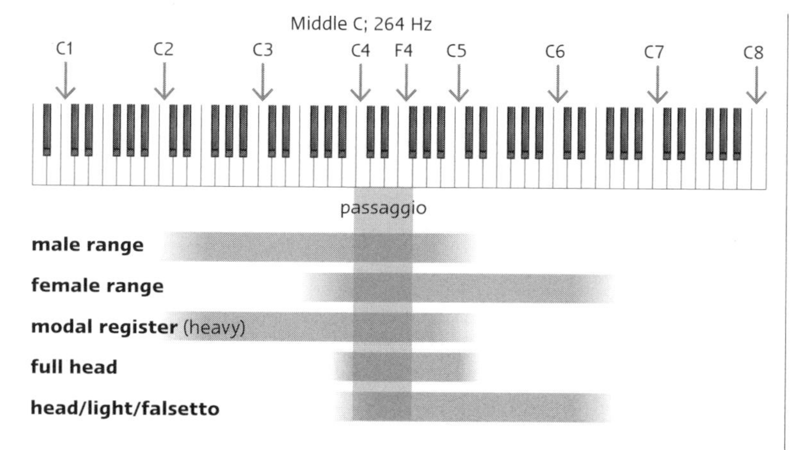

The male voice has roughly two octaves below and one octave above the passaggio. With the female voice it's the other way around: It has one octave below, and two octaves above the passaggio.

register. These terms prevent confusion with what's known as chest resonance and help avoid the idea of the voice coming out of the chest.

Head, light, or falsetto

The register above the passaggio is often referred to as the *head register* for female singers, and as *falsetto* for male singers. Others use falsetto or *light register* for both the male and the female voice.

Full head or middle

There is a limited range in which you can choose between using your heavy or your light register. Some don't consider this a separate register, but rather a variation on the modal register, using the names head or full head. Others identify it as a separate middle register or head register.

Lighter

In this range, your timbre is in between both registers: It's lighter than in the heavy register, yet not as light as in your high register.

Not fast enough

At the top end of this range, you have to switch to your light, head or falsetto register: In their 'modal mode,' your vocal folds simply can't vibrate fast enough to generate high notes. The very highest notes some vocalists can sing before switching are usually said

to be around C5–D5. Most singers have to switch a lot sooner, though.

Speaking voices

Both men and women usually speak in their heavy register. Most men speak at a pitch around A2; women about an octave higher, around A3, just below Middle C.

Men

Most men sing in their heavy register too, both in classical and in non-classical music. They have a range of about two octaves in this register, below the passaggio. The only classical male voice to consistently use the falsetto register is the *counter tenor* (see page 101).

Women

For women, it's different. Non-classical singers predominantly sing in their heavy register. This generates a very natural sound, and makes for intelligible lyrics. Classical singers mainly sing in their light or falsetto register, giving the voice a completely different, classical timbre.

Tipcode VOCALS-014
This Tipcode demonstrates the sound of a non-classical (male) falsetto.

Falsetto

Traditionally, the term *falsetto* was reserved for classical male singers. For women, this register was referred to as the head register. Today, there's a growing tendency to use the same register names for both men and women. After all, the physiological difference between the two main registers is identical for both genders.

One register

The break or passaggio is one of the most dreaded aspects of the human voice. There are various ways to deal with it (see pages 92–94). One way is to approach the voice as a one-register instrument: If there's just one register, there is no break. Introducing registers creates fear of the passaggio, which will often increase the risk of an audible 'break.'

Non-classical falsetto

Both male and female singers use their falsetto register in non-classical singing too. Some male singers do so most or all the time (*e.g.*, the Bee Gees); others use it as an effect. The non-classical falsetto sounds quite different from the classically trained falsetto voice.

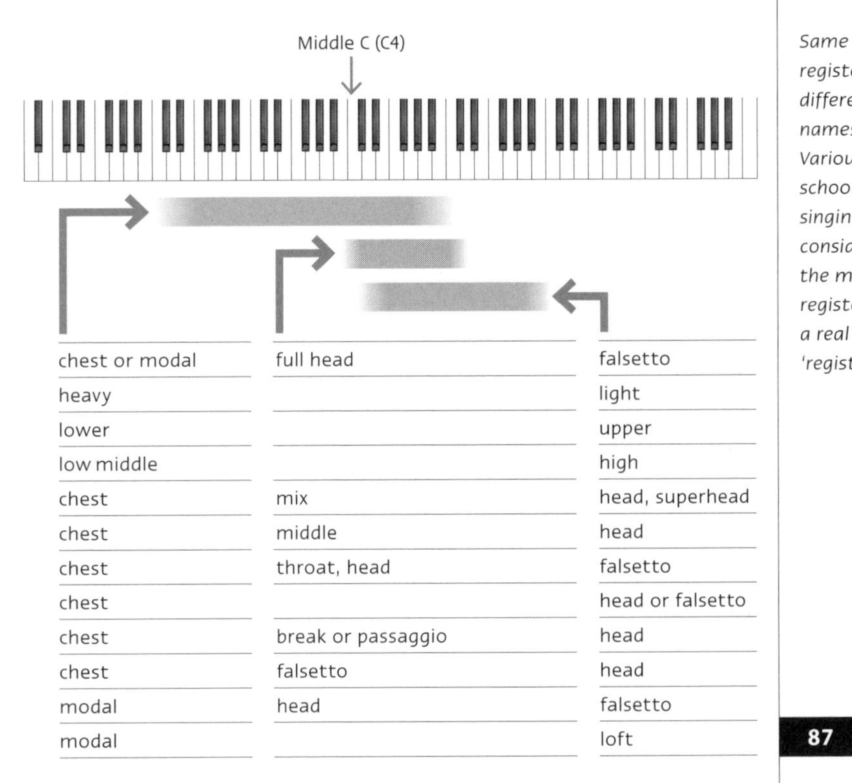

chest or modal	full head	falsetto
heavy		light
lower		upper
low middle		high
chest	mix	head, superhead
chest	middle	head
chest	throat, head	falsetto
chest		head or falsetto
chest	break or passaggio	head
chest	falsetto	head
modal	head	falsetto
modal		loft

Same registers, different names. Various schools of singing don't consider the middle register a real 'register.'

Bridges

Another approach is to use a completely different terminology, talking about *areas of resonation* rather than registers, and about *bridges* rather than breaks.

Two or three

In the end, most schools of thought distinguish two or three main registers. The confusion about the subject is caused mainly by the many different ways used to indicate these registers, as shown in the table on the previous page.

Falsetto or head register?

The terms head register and falsetto are the most frequently discussed. Some experts use them interchangeably. Others feel that the head voice and the falsetto voice, specifically in male singers, are two distinct registers complete with their own characteristics, the head voice producing overtones and possessing a ring that the falsetto does not; the falsetto produces few overtones and lacks the singer's formant. There are also experts who disapprove of the term falsetto, or who disapprove of singing in falsetto altogether, simply stating that it sounds awful and that it will ruin your voice.

REGISTERS AND TIMBRE

No matter how many registers you think there are or how you name them, there is a clear timbre difference between your lowest notes and your highest notes. One of the main goals for most singers is to create an even timbre over their entire range: Compared to your low notes, your high notes shouldn't sound as if they're sung by someone else. Also, you should be able to sing any scale, up and down, and cross the passaggio as seamlessly as possible, without serious breaks or disruptions.

Different vibrations

The distinctly different timbres of your two main registers result from the different ways your vocal folds vibrate in each register.

Explaining these complex differences in detail would take another book — so here are the basics:

Tipcode VOCALS-015

Angela demonstrates the distinctly different timbres of the two main registers.

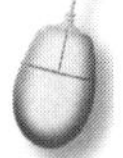

Heavy

In the heavy register, the entire 'mass' of your vocal folds is involved. The folds are short, with little tension, and they're thick and slack. Singing higher notes is a matter of raising the internal tension of the vocal folds, *i.e.*, the tension of the *musculus vocalis* in each fold.

Light

The light register has a quite different timbre: lighter, thinner, with less body, and a smaller dynamic range. The *musculi vocales* are inactive. Only the edges of the vocal folds vibrate. Singing a higher note is a matter of stretching the vocal folds.

Figures

There's yet another difference: the *closed quotient.* In your heavy register the glottis is actually closed more than 50% of the duration of each cycle (glottis opens, puff of air escapes, glottis closes). An example: When you sing E4, a cycle lasts 3 milliseconds. In your heavy register, you glottis will then be closed for 1.5 milliseconds or more during each cycle. In the high register, the glottis is closed for less than 40% of the duration of each cycle. It also opens less wide than it does in the heavy register.

One or the other

The two modes of vibration of the vocal folds cannot be mixed:

Tipcode VOCALS-016
Singing E4 (332 hertz), your vocal folds open 332 times per second — no matter which vowel you sing.

They vibrate either one way, or the other. The area in which you can choose to use either one of these modes is sometimes referred to as the middle register or full head register — though it's actually a 'light' version of the heavy, modal register. The lighter timbre is a result of slight differences in the ways the vocal folds open and close the glottis. Also, the vocal folds are a bit more taut — yet not stretched, as they are in falsetto.

Mixed voice?

According to this theory (based on scientific research among pro and amateur singers, classical and contemporary) there's no such thing as a *mixed voice*. Other schools of thought do use that term, though, indicating the same general area between the heavy and light registers. The expression 'mixed voice' is also used in other ways (see page 96).

Determine your range

To find out the range that you can sing both in your heavy and your light register, sing from your lowest note up, note for note, until you have to go into your light register. Remember that note: It's the highest note of this range. Then start high, and go down, note for note, until you have to go into your heavy (chest or modal) register. That note is the lowest note of your full head or 'middle' register.

A bit more air

To hear the timbre difference between your heavy (modal) and middle (full head) register, try singing a note that you can sing both ways. This will probably be a note around Middle C. Sing it 'from the chest' at first, and then sing it in your middle register by 'giving it some extra air' — without making it sound breathy.

Registers and timbre

A final note: Each register has its own, specific timbre, but of course you can influence your timbre in each register. You can sound bright in your chest register, or sad in falsetto, and so on (see Resonance and timbre, page 54).

EXTREME REGISTERS

There are more registers than the ones mentioned above. Two extreme registers are the *vocal fry* at the very low end of the male range, and the *whistle register* at the top end of the female range.

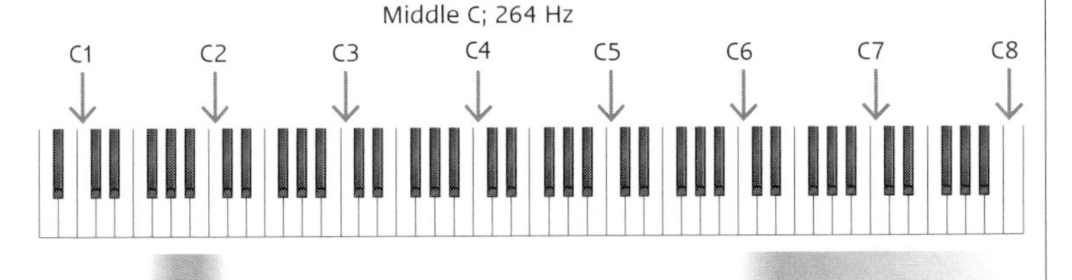

The two extreme registers: the vocal fry or growl register and the whistle or bell register.

Vocal fry

At frequencies lower than some 70Hz (around C#2) the voice starts to sound as if you can count the separate jets of air that escape through the glottis. Some of the names that illustrate the sound of this low register are *vocal fry, glottal fry, growl register, growl bass, pulse register, vocal rattle*, and *vocal scrape*. In classical literature you may also find the German terms *Strohbass* and *Schnarrbass*. As you can see, the number of names for this rarely used register easily exceeds the very small number of notes it encompasses.

Whistle

The whistle register, *bell register*, or *flute register* is a bit less unusual, but you won't hear it every day either. There are few female singers who can effectively use this register. It's so high that lyrics can't be sung, and all you hear is a high, flute-like tone. The timbre is usually quite shallow, though a few singers manage to add some depth and color to it.

B5 and up

The whistle register starts around B5 or C6. Opinions on the highest note of the flute register differ. Some say it's around F6, others say C7 or even C8 (the highest note on a piano, at more than 4,200Hz!).

Male whistle?

Though the flute register is usually considered exclusive to the female voice, some use it for the very highest range of the male voice (and others call *that* falsetto!).

PASSAGGIO

The passaggio is where you switch between your main registers. Most singers try to seamlessly connect or unify these registers, equalizing their different timbres. The passaggio is also known as the *break*, *register transition*, *register change*, *gear change*, or *bridge*.

Don't think about it

Just as thinking about singing in tune can make you sing out of tune, thinking too much about the passaggio can make it trouble you more than it should.

No clue

There are singers who haven't got a clue what a passaggio is, because they've never been bothered by it. Generally speaking, female singers are troubled less by the passaggio than male singers, and it's easier for them to learn to equalize their voice.

Lighter timbre, less trouble

Likewise, singers with a lighter timbre seem to have less trouble than those with a darker timbre: Basses usually have a harder time learning to bridge the break than tenors. The difference in timbre between the highest notes of their heavy register and the lowest notes of their light register is much bigger too.

Same area

As said before, the passaggio occurs in the same general area for almost all voices, between C4 and F4. For basses and altos it's usually around D4. For baritones and sopranos it can be a bit higher, around E4; for tenors it's often around E4–F4.

Extending the modal register

The modal register can be extended, however. A tenor is expected to be able to sing C5 before switching, and non-classical female singers to D5, or even higher (belting; see page 95).

Automatic shift

The passaggio can be shifted consciously, but it can also shift as a result of the vowel you sing, the loudness of your tone, or the direction you sing in — going up or down in pitch.

- If you sing a closed vowel (*i.e.*, a vowel that requires a small mouth opening: *i* or *u*) the passaggio tends to occur at a lower pitch. Singing an open vowel, such as an *ah*, can make the passaggio move upward as much as a minor third (*i.e.*, from D to F).
- If you sing loud, the register transition tends to move up.
- In an ascending melody, the passaggio typically occurs at a higher pitch than when you sing a descending melody.
- The register transition can also change from day to day, and it can be lower in the morning than it is later that same day. Practice routines throughout the day can help you discover — and control — these differences.

Check?

To check the above, just sing scales that include the passaggio, using different vowels each time, singing louder and softer, and moving up and down the scale.

Control

Of course, you can also learn to control where the passaggio occurs, so you can move it up or down a bit, avoiding this area as you sing.

Pushing it up

If you overdo this, you may be in trouble. Pushing the passaggio up in an attempt to extend your heavy or middle register may damage your voice. It's much like singing in a range that's not yours. However, there are ways to extend your registers without any problems, as you will see below.

Exercises

There are many different exercises to learn how to equalize the passaggio, eliminating the break. These exercises range from singing glides (sliding exercises) to singing short scales (each next one half a step up: first C, D, E, F, G; then C♯, D♯, F, F♯, G♯; etc.) that include the passaggio.

Tipcode VOCALS-017
Singing short scales to equalize the passaggio.

More than one

Some singing methods speak of two, three, four, or even five passaggios — but the goal is always to connect, unify, or blend the different registers that they may separate.
Do note that other methods don't mention the passaggio at all...

BELTING

Some styles of music require loud, high notes, and intelligible lyrics. The answer is a technique called belting.

Tipcode VOCALS-018

Play Tipcode VOCALS-018 to hear a brief demonstration of belting.

Not just Broadway

Belting is often associated with female vocalists in Broadway style musicals, but belting is also utilized in many other styles of music, from gospel to rock, pop, jazz, and international folk music.

And men too

While some experts state that belting is strictly a female thing, others say that there are plenty of male belters too, from Al Jolson to Bill Haley and even Frank Sinatra.

A register?

Belting is a technique, not a register. However, since it has so much to do with extending the lower register, it is discussed in this chapter.

Many definitions

There are many ways to define belting. For example, it has been described as singing from the belt, singing loud without damage, or simply as high-energy singing, using terms such as loud projection, tough, driving, assertive, brassy, and yelling. In all applications, vibrato is limited.

Strong and high

Belting is singing with strong breath support, a lot of air, and a high larynx to increase projection and loudness. Some experts also add a certain type of formant tuning (see page 63) to their definition. As a result, what some call belting, others don't.

Driving it up

The word 'belting' has a forceful connotation involving the need to drive your voice over a certain point, or to forcefully push the limits of your lower register. It seems to be mainly for this reason that some experts warn against this technique, stating that it will ruin your voice. Others just don't like the word itself for the same reason, and they use different names for the same technique. *Mixed voice* is one of them — adding to the confusion.

C5 and up

Warning signals against belting often come from classical schools of singing, where it's generally unusual for female singers to use the heavy register at all, and extremely unusual to extend its range beyond E4. However, *high belters* can go as high as C5, D5, or even E5! *Low belters* sing up to about G4.

Riskier

The combination of a high energy level, a high larynx, and high notes does require a lot of control and proper technique. Belting poorly may be riskier than less demanding styles of singing — but there are various singing methods (see Chapter 7) that offer great tools to help you learn this technique.

Legit voices

Belting has always been related to the Broadway musical theater shows. Often, these shows also have female roles that require a more classical, falsetto, or head type of sound. Broadway singers call these legit *or* legitimate voices. *These voices are different from the traditional operatic voices, though, if only for the fact that lyrics are more important in musical theatre shows.*

6

Voice Types and Ranges

Just like some musical instruments — saxophones, for example — singers are classified according to their range and timbre. These classifications are mainly used in classical singing and in choirs, but other singers may benefit from knowing a bit about the subject too. The second part of this chapter offers related information on the range of the singing voice, how it's determined, and whether it can be extended.

There is of course a major difference between classifying saxophones and classifying the human voice: Saxophones are manufactured in set sizes with set ranges. Humans aren't. There are typical bass voices, and typical soprano singers, and so on, but there are many singers whose voices fall anywhere between the main categories. A vocal teacher or a choir director can help you determine the type of voice you have.

Comfortable

Your voice type is mainly determined by the range you can most comfortably sing in — the range in which your voice sounds best, and in which you have most control over it, with good dynamics (the capacity to sing both softly and loudly), power, musicality, conviction, and, for classical singers, projection or 'ring.'

Extreme notes

So it's not about the very lowest and the very highest notes you can sing. These extreme notes are hardly ever usable on stage. Your actual working range is much smaller.

Why?

Why is it important to know which voice type you have? Because it tells you about your working range, and because singing outside of this range can be harmful, or make singing less fun.

Timbre

Your timbre also plays an important role in determining your voice type. A baritone may very well be able to sing the same range as a typical bass, but the baritone has a lighter timbre.

Overlap

The illustration below clearly shows that the ranges of the various voice types overlap. Even the very lowest male and the very highest female voices have a common range of a fourth, or even an octave, if you include the highest notes of the bass.

Different

Of course, if a bass sings Middle C, it sounds very different from a soprano singing the same note: Middle C is in the top range of the bass, and in the bottom range of the soprano. And if the bass sings the octave above Middle C, things will sound very different again.

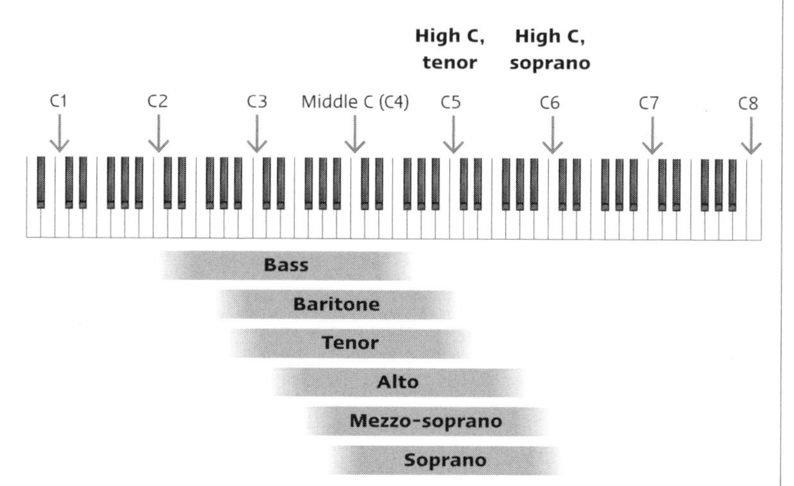

Average ranges of various types of voice.

Tipcode VOCALS-019

The same note — yet with a distinctly different timbre.

The main types of voice

The four main types of voice are bass, tenor, alto, and soprano: a lower and a higher male voice, and a lower and a higher female voice. These are not the only ones, though. There's also the contralto, the mezzo-soprano, and the baritone, for example.

Exact notes?

In many books on singing, the ranges of the various types of voice are indicated with note names. As you will see, however, opinions differ on what the exact lowest and highest notes for each type of voice are. For example, some say the range of a tenor is from E3 to C5, while others add another fifth to this range, starting as low as A2. Likewise, the range of mezzo-sopranos is said to end at A5, or C6, or even higher. In the illustration on the previous page, note names have been left out in order not to add to the confusion.

An octave

The difference between the lowest male and female voices (bass and contralto) is about an octave, and so is the difference between the highest male and female voices. Likewise, High C for a tenor is C5; High C for a soprano is C6, an octave higher. Note that the speaking voices of men and women are about an octave apart too!

Most singers

Most male singers, both in classical and non-classical music, are baritones. The range and timbre of this voice type are between those of the bass and the tenor. In non-classical Western music, most female singers are altos, contraltos, or mezzo-sopranos.

Lack of tenors

There tends to be a lack of tenors in many choirs. As a result, baritones, preferably those with a relatively light timbre, are often asked to sing the tenor parts. In other choirs, altos are asked to do the same. As said before, however, singing outside of your range, or even singing at the top of your range most of the time, is not without risk. Having singers sing in a range that's not completely theirs is not the best way to create a good-sounding choir either.

First and second

In choirs, the main sections are often divided into two smaller groups, *e.g.*, the *first altos* (higher) and the *second altos* (lower).

Opera

In opera, voice classification is even more diversified: There are some twenty-five different voice types. The very highest operatic voice is the *coloratura soprano*, a very light, flexible voice with a range up to F6.At the other extreme is the *basso serioso* ('serious bass'). If you want to hear both extremes in one opera, listen to Mozart's Die *Zauberflöte* (*The Magic Flute*).

Lyric, dramatic, buffo, spinto

Opera subdivides some of the main voice types in more precise categories. For example, sopranos and tenors can be either *lyric* or *dramatic*. Lyric voices have a lighter, flexible, versatile timbre; the dramatic type sounds darker and heavier. Some other extensions are *buffo* ('comical' voice), and *spinto* (a tad darker than lyric).

Right voice for the role

In most movies, you can easily tell the good guys from the bad guys, and the rich from the poor. In the opera, you can just as easily hear those differences: The hero, for example, is often performed by a heroic tenor. Likewise, the countess will have a weightier voice than her chambermaid, even if they're both sopranos.

Counter tenor

Counter tenors are male singers who consistently sing in their falsetto register. Their range is typically from G3 to G5, and sometimes even up to C6, the alto's High C. They often sing the parts of the *castratos* in the Renaissance and Baroque music of the seventeenth and eighteenth centuries, even though they do have a different timbre. There's more about castrato singers in Chapter 11.

Altus: a male alto

Many experts prefer to use the term *altus* rather than counter tenor, to clearly indicate that it's a male alto, rather than a tenor.

Voice type and age

The human voice tends to get darker with age. As a result, singers may have to switch from, say, the lyric roles they sing in the beginning of their careers, to dramatic roles later on.

RANGES

Your vocal folds, the size of your larynx, and other elements of your vocal instrument determine both your timbre and your range. Good voice lessons may add one or more notes to your range, or at least help improve your control over your highest and lowest notes, and their timbre.

How long?

Male voices mainly sound lower because male vocal folds are longer. Male vocal folds are usually up to some 0.9" (22 mm) in length; female folds are some 0.4" (10 mm) shorter. You may find slightly different figures in other books, depending on how the folds are measured.

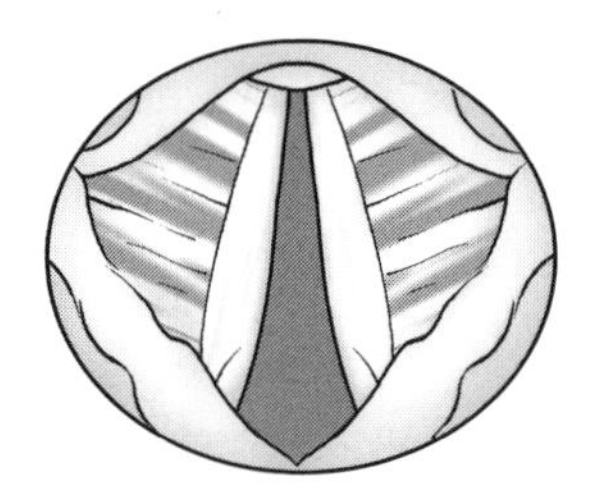

Male vocal folds in actual size.

Heavy or light

Differences in the mass of the vocal folds plays a role too: Heavier folds may generate lower pitches than lighter folds. They make for a darker timbre as well. Lighter folds enhance the lyrical qualities of a voice.

Tension

Your range also has to do with the inherent tension of the vocal folds. If you have a low-pitched voice, your vocal folds have a low intrinsic tension.

Larynx

The size of the larynx is another element that determines your range. The male larynx, with its pointed Adam's apple, is deeper than the female larynx. Exact figures vary, as usual, but the difference is about a quarter of an inch.

No match

In some cases, the various dimensions of a vocal instrument don't match. You may have a baritone timbre but a tenor pitch, for example. This can limit your possibilities in classical music. In non-classical music, you can usually match the music you sing to the voice you have.

Careful judgment

Of course, voice classification is not a matter of taking measurements, but of careful judgment by a teacher, a choir director, or another expert.

Large range, small range

As a singer, you're better off with a small range and a good voice, than with a huge range and a voice that nobody cares to listen to. As the illustration on page 99 shows, the normal range for each type of voice is some 2.5 to 3 octaves. There are singers with larger ranges, but they're rare.

Non-classical singers can get by with a much smaller range, selecting songs that can be performed within that range only, or arranging them so that they can.

Different keys

Most popular songs, from jazz to rock, can be performed with a range of an octave and a half, and there are many that don't span more than an octave.

So can you do with a range that small? Yes, you actually can, but extending your range will definitely allow you to sing songs in a wider variety of keys. Having some extra high and low notes available also allows you to add extra touches or effects to a song, making it more personal.

Classical music too

Most classical music doesn't require you to sing over a wider range than an octave and a half either — but the notes that are required above and below that range are often essential.

Expanding your range

How much your range can be extended depends on your natural range. Some untrained singers have a very small range that can be expanded half an octave or more. Others have a naturally large range, which cannot be extended in terms of adding new notes — but you can always work on improving the stability of the extreme notes. Practicing to the extreme ends of your range also helps to make the other notes sound more natural.

Higher or lower

Expanding the range is usually a matter of adding notes to the top end. Many singers know that their range is extended downward in the morning: When you wake up, you'll probably be able to sing lower notes than you can a little later. The ultra low notes are the result of complete relaxation of your vocal folds. The slacker they are, the lower the pitch they can produce.

No range

Also, there are singers who have a much narrower range in the morning. Getting your vocal folds back to work often requires a warm-up (see page 118).

Non-classical singers

If you ask ten female non-classical singers to sing a song in their favorite key, most of them will start around the same pitch. Ask ten male non-classical singers the same question, and one may start as much as an octave higher or lower than the next. How come? Both male and female non-classical singers mostly sing in their heavy register, and female singers simply have a much smaller range in that register (one octave, instead of two), so they have less to choose from.

Children

Children have very short vocal folds, and their ranges are usually very limited: A boy's range is typically from about A3 to A4, and most girls can sing from about D4 to D5.

What will they be?

A child's voice is an unreliable indicator of his or her future voice type. A boy with a low voice can become a tenor; girls with high voices may be classified as altos later on. Likewise, young children that sing terribly out of tune when they're really young (under eight), may come out as good singers — unless they're discouraged from singing because they don't sound great from the start.

7

Singing Methods

The information and the terminology provided in the previous chapters is in part based on the classical or bel canto approach of the vocal instrument, which dates back to the late sixteenth century, or even the Middle Ages. In later years, new methods of (teaching) singing, and new approaches of the singing voice have been developed. The following chapter offers a brief overview of some of these methods.

One of the main differences between more recent methods of singing and the classical, bel canto approach is that the latter focuses on one specified ideal of sound — a flexible, agile, and lyric timbre that is even throughout its entire range; a type of sound that is perfect for opera stages, for example, but that may not work so well for rock or jazz singers. That said, many vocalists in these and other styles have had and still have great teachers with a classical background.

Not just one

This Tipbook can, but will not, tell you which singing method you should choose, if any. It's probably wisest to explore more than one of them, and see which elements best suit you, your voice, and your style of singing. The teacher you choose is an important element in this choice: Teachers with the same theoretical background may approach singing and their students in very different ways.

Non-classical styles

One of the main common elements in more recent singing methods is that they claim to be suited for any type of voice and any style of singing, from classical to heavy metal, and jazz, rather than being opposed to certain styles of singing that — from the bel canto point of view — would be harmful for your voice (or just plain awful, compared to the 'ideal' sound). Another element that these methods have in common is that they're all said to be based on thorough, scientific research of the vocal instrument.

EVTS

Singer/recitalist Jo Estill, who researched the human voice for over thirty years, is the founder of the Estill Voice Training System (EVTS) or Estill Voice Craft. This system teaches vocalists and others a number of structures that help them control a series of voice related muscle combinations. A clear understanding of how the voice works is an important basis for EVTS.

Levels

EVTS has two levels. Level one, known as Compulsory Figures For Voice, encompasses the structures mentioned above. Level two is an application of these structures in practice, leading to the six types of voice sounds or voice qualities that EVTS distinguishes:

- Speech (used in jazz, pop, Broadway, and other styles)
- Falsetto (a breathy timbre, as used by the Bee Gees, or in Broadway musical theatre shows)
- Sob (a low, dark timbre: jazz, classical singing, opera)
- Twang (brassy, very bright: country, Broadway, opera, pop)
- Opera
- Belting (happy yelling to music, in EVTS terms: funk, gospel, Broadway, pop)

Master teachers

EVTS is said to help you to expand your range and perform in any musical style, to create a wide variety of sounds, and to avoid vocal trauma. It can be used to teach singers at any age and in any style. exclusively. Books on EVTS are available only through Certified Master Teachers (CMT).

More information

For more information, please check out www.evts.com and www.trainmyvoice.com.

CVT

The Danish singer and teacher Cathrine Sadolin, who has performed and taught both in classical and non-classical settings, developed Complete Vocal Technique based on her own research of the vocal instrument.

Four subjects

Her Complete Vocal Technique (CVT) is a method that can be used for singers in any style, allowing them to healthily produce any type of sound. CVT has four main subjects:

- The three basic principles
- Four modes
- Sound color
- Effects

Three basic principles

The three basic principles of CVT are an open throat (avoiding constrictions in the vocal instrument), proper support, and 'avoiding a protruded jaw and tensions in the lips,' as stated in Sadolin's book *Complete Vocal Technique* (see page 214). Obeying these three principles enables singers to use their entire range and produce a clear and powerful sound, while preventing symptoms such as hoarseness.

Four modes

CVT distinguishes four vocal modes, which differ in how 'metallic' they are. These four modes are Neutral, Curbing, Overdrive, and Belting. Neutral is known as the non-metallic mode. This mode is used when you sing a lullaby, for example, but also for all female classical singing in the high range of the voice. CVT describes Curbing as 'a half metallic mode, with a slight edge on the notes. Curbing is the mildest of the metallic modes.' The Overdrive mode is fully metallic. This mode is used when you speak or sing loudly. The sound of belting, the fourth mode, is described as 'light, aggressive, sharp and screaming'. Incidentally, it should be noted that the CVT and EVTS definitions of the word 'belting' are very different.

Sound color

Within these modes you can go for a lighter or darker timbre or sound color by controlling the vocal tract, *e.g.*, by changing the position of your larynx or the shape of your tongue.

Effects

When you're able to control the three basic principles, the modes, and the sound color, you may use a variety of effects, ranging from distortion and growl to vocal breaks and vibrato. CVT differs from other methods by clearly defining a large number of effects, and Sadolin strongly believes that 'it is possible to produce ALL sounds in a healthy manner' without damaging the vocal instrument.

More information

For more information, please visit www.completevocaltechnique.

com. The quotes in the paragraphs above were taken from the pages of this site, which also supplies information on the CVT singer and singer/teacher courses, including online lessons.

SPEECH LEVEL SINGING

Speech Level Singing, like bel canto (Italian for 'beautiful singing'), is considered a classical or 'legit' singing technique. The method, developed by Seth Riggs, is claimed to be effective for singers in any style of music, from opera to folk, and jazz..

Basic principles

Two of the basic principles of Speech Level Singing (SLS) are that the larynx stays low and still as you sing, and that the vocal folds stay together over the entire range of your voice.
Speech Level Singing focuses on training of the vocal cords in order to get the most out of your vocal instrument while preventing symptoms.

Levels

SLS works with teachers at five different levels. Lessons and coaching are provided in various ways, ranging from private teachers and SLS camps to master classes and lessons via the phone.

More information

More information on SLS can be found at www. speechlevelsinging.com. This site also provides contact information for certified SLS teachers around the world.

OTHER METHODS

There are many more methods of singing, such as:

- the Lichtenberger Method (www.lichtenberger-institut.de), taught at the German Lichtenberg Institute for Applied Physiology of the Voice only;
- Perfect Voice (www.perfect-voice.com), based on the research of Professor Feuchtinger;
- Ultimate Voice Training, a home study program (www.voicetraining.com/).

Please check out their websites for additional information, and check the list of recommended literature on pages 214–216 of this Tipbook.

Voice Care

The singing voice is a very vulnerable instrument. It's also the only instrument that can't be replaced if it breaks, and there are no spare ones available. The only way to enjoy a healthy voice as much and as long as you can is to take proper care of it.

The first section of this chapter covers things you can do to prevent vocal health problems. The second section deals with some well-known voice problems and what you can do about them. These sections overlap quite often: What you can do to cure voice problems is often what you could have done to prevent them.

What (not) to do

The first section of this chapter may seem like a list of do's and don'ts, but it's not. Just refer to it when you have problems: You may find what caused them, or how to solve them.

More

The more you sing, the more you probably should do to maintain your vocal instrument. If you sing for an hour twice a week, there's probably no reason to adapt your diet or other habits — though even this little extra vocal energy may throw your vocal system off balance.

Suddenly

Likewise, voice problems can suddenly pop up as a result of something you've been doing for years. Smoking, for example, or drinking milk, to name something seemingly far more innocent.

Water and rest

Water and rest often seem to be the two main things when it comes to voice care, prevention, and recovery from a wide variety of voice problems. Water is readily available, cheap, and beneficial for more than just your voice. Rest can be more elusive — not only for professional singers, but also for people working in other jobs that demand a lot of vocal activity (e.g., teachers, sales persons). Still, rest can do things that medication can't — so you may just have to.

PREVENTION

Drink plenty of water, allow your vocal folds sufficient rest, learn good vocal technique, speak well, breathe properly, quit smoking,

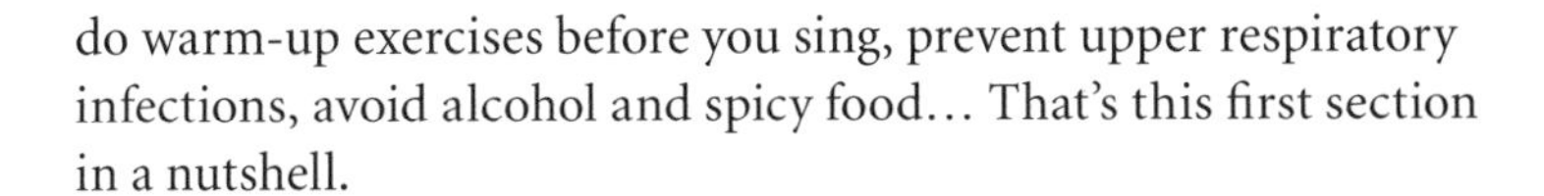

do warm-up exercises before you sing, prevent upper respiratory infections, avoid alcohol and spicy food… That's this first section in a nutshell.

Eat healthily

If you don't eat healthily, there's not much else you can do to keep your voice healthy. There's no need for a special diet; just make sure your food contains sufficient amounts of vitamins, minerals, and so on. When in doubt, you may want to consult a dietician.

Full or empty stomach

Singing can be as hard on a full stomach as on an empty one. It's often recommended to eat no later than two or three hours before a performance. Note that certain types of food digest a lot quicker than others.

Water

One of the few things singers from all backgrounds agree upon is that you should drink plenty of water, plenty meaning three to five pints, or two to three liters, a day. You can tell you've been drinking enough water when your urine is pale. Water is also the best thing to drink onstage and during intermissions.

Room temperature

Preferably drink water at room temperature, without ice: Your vocal folds don't appreciate hot and cold drinks. Many singers prefer mineral water.

Inhaler

Some singers use a steam inhaler, but most only do so when they're having problems, or after singing in a room with a lot of smokers. Aroma-therapeutic oils can be added to the water.

Humidifiers

If you sleep with your mouth open and frequently wake up with a dry throat, it might be wise to install a humidifier in your bedroom. If possible, keep a window open for fresh air. Air conditioning systems lower the humidity level!

Rest

Vocal rest is often mandatory when you're suffering from vocal problems, but it can help prevent them too. Refrain from talking too much after a performance, for instance, and have a good night's sleep. Also, try not to talk too much before a performance.

Onstage

Give your voice some rest onstage. Consciously relax your vocal instrument when you don't sing (intermission, guitar solo, instrumental song), breathe well, and try not to talk too much between sets, especially if you have to compete with the music that's played in the intermission.

Two weeks

Too much rest can have ill effects too. Some singers can start singing right away after two weeks of vacation and vocal rest; others have to build their voices up slowly if they don't want to hurt themselves. Many — professional — singers keep on practicing while on vacation.

Technique

One of the best ways to prevent voice problems is to develop good technique. Untrained singing is one of the main causes for hoarseness, sore throats, and other problems. Good vocal technique can even eradicate symptoms, ranging from headaches to backaches and breathing deficiencies.

Strong voice

Some people have stronger voices than others. Strong voices don't suffer from dehydration, overuse, milk, alcohol, or smoking as much or as fast as weaker voices do, and they tend to recover faster when something does go wrong. But strength can be misleading too, and even the strongest voice can suffer sudden and unexpected damage.

Speaking well

Various vocal problems can result from not using your speaking voice properly. Many people, singers and non-singers, speak at a pitch that's too low for their vocal instrument. If your speaking voice doesn't sound clear, chances are you're one of them. Others speak higher than their optimal speaking pitch. If you think you fit into one of these categories, check with a speech therapist.

Too loudly, too softly

It's evident that talking too loudly can upset your voice, so you may want to avoid noisy parties, bars, clubs, and other places where you have to raise your voice. Yelling is even worse. Talking too softly can be just as harmful: Whispering is often said to be bad for your voice (see page 123)!

Your range

Avoid singing out of your range, or singing at the extremes of your range for too long. Match the music to your voice, if possible (see page 72). If you sing in a choir, make sure that you're in the right section: Proper voice classification is essential.

Your voice

Get to know your voice, and how you sound, rather than trying to emulate the voice of your favorite singer. Avoid singing louder than you should. If your voice gets lost against the volume of the other singers in a choir, consult the director or a teacher. And if you can't hear your voice in a band mix, don't just turn up the monitor level. (See page 73 instead.)

Breathe well

Several breathing techniques were discussed on page 40. Don't apply these tips only when you sing. Breathing well all day long can prevent various vocal problems, and it has a positive effect on your stress level.

Stress and rage

Emotional health is important for singers too. Stress, anxiety, tension, insecurity, sorrow, rage, and frustration can cause a wide range of vocal problems, from singing out of tune to a sore throat.

Don't smoke

Smoking dehydrates, it irritates the lining of your vocal instrument, it can cause swelling of your vocal folds, and various lethal diseases. Smoking marijuana is even worse (besides being illegal), for one thing because it burns at higher temperatures.

Some smoke

Some singers do not give up smoking because they believe it gives their voice a specific quality. It probably does — but it's a high price to pay.

Don't cough

Smoking will make you cough too, and so do many other irritants, from powdered sugar, animal hair, and dusty stage floors to a cold that leaves excess mucous or phlegm on your vocal folds. Coughing is detrimental to your vocal folds: To cough, you bring them together tightly and then let them 'explode' all of a sudden, as in a major glottal attack. This harmful explosion is intended to shake the foreign substances or mucous from the vocal folds. You'd do better humming it off. See page 125 for more information on this technique.

Artificial smoke

If there's artificial smoke onstage, try to avoid inhaling it.

Checkup

If you sing a lot, it can't hurt to visit an ENT-specialist (ear-, nose-, throat-specialist, a.k.a. otolaryngologist) for a periodic checkup, just to make sure all is well.

Warm-up

Singing is high-energy sport for your vocal folds and your larynx. Consistently warming up your vocal instrument prior to singing can help prevent a lot of problems, and it will boost your vocal development.

Wake up, warm-up

There are many different warm-up exercises. For amateur singers, it can be enough to do some of these exercises before each practice session and each performance. Professional singers will often do more.

At breakfast or in the shower

Some consider breakfast the first warm-up of the day. Chewing and swallowing are said to be great ways to get your vocal apparatus to wake up. Other singers start in the shower, warming up the voice with humming and other low energy exercises. Sighing in various parts of your range is another effective morning warm-up.

An hour or ten minutes

How long you should warm up before a performance or a rehearsal depends on many things. Some experts say a ten-minute warm-up will usually do; others will tell you to spend at least an hour. Professional singers are likely to warm up longer than amateur choir members. When you get older, you may find you need to warm up longer.

Hum, zzz, slide, and trill

Popular warm-up exercises include humming, singing long voiced consonants (zzz, vvv), singing scales and pitch glides, lip trills, messa di voce (see page 30), and all kinds of vocalizing exercises. Always start slowly and at a comfortable pitch, and work your way up from there. There are plenty of books that offer more detail

Tipcode VOCALS-020

Here are some examples of classic warm-up exercises.

on vocal exercises. Also consider consulting a teacher to find out what's best for you: Books don't know you.

Tapes

Rather than humming and singing at random, many singers like to use warm-up tapes or CDs with various sequences of warm-up exercises, scales, and so on.

Cool down

Similar exercises are applied to cool down (or warm down, as others say) the voice after a concert.

Your body

Many singers do more than vocal exercises alone. They also loosen their tongue and their jaw, massaging the latter; they relax their head, shoulders, back, ribs, arms, and legs; some do yoga stretches. The less tension there is in your body, the better you may sound.

Warming up

If your voice hurts, it's best not to sing. But if you have to, don't skip your warm-up. Warming up may take longer, but singing with a 'cold' voice in bad condition will definitely increase the damage.

Food and drinks

For some singers, a bar of chocolate or a glass of milk is enough to ruin their voice; others can digest a heavy, spicy meal, have ice

Avoid URIs

Non-singers probably try to avoid laryngitis, sinusitis, and other upper respiratory infections (URIs) as much as singers do: They're not only bad for your voice, but they make you feel lousy allover. As soon as you feel a URI coming up, it can't hurt to drink extra water and maybe add a nutritional supplement to your diet. Let your pharmacist or another expert advise you. If you frequently suffer from URIs, consult a physician.

cream for dessert, and still sing well. Here are some examples of types of food and beverages that may hinder your singing.

- Your vocal folds don't like hot and cold drinks. Again, **room temperature water is best**. No ice!
- **Lemon juice** can help you get rid of mucous, but it can also irritate your throat.
- **Heavy meals**, and that includes most types of fast food, don't promote good singing.
- **Spicy foods** can irritate your vocal folds and increase the amount of acid in your stomach, which is bad news if you suffer from gastric reflux (see page 127). Alcohol, chocolate, coffee, (non-herbal) tea and sodas can have the same effect.
- **Nuts and powdered sugar** can make you cough, and coughing is bad for your vocal folds.
- **Dairy products** (including cheese and chocolate) can increase the production of mucous.
- **Orange juice, alcohol, and sugar** can have the same effect, and for some people bread can too. Note that many types of food and drink contain sugar, and some cough and throat lozenges do too.
- **Alcohol** dehydrates, especially the next day, and it can cause swelling of the vocal folds. Alcohol can also numb your senses, making you unaware of the fact that you're singing too loud, or for too long. Combining alcohol and cigarettes is probably the worst thing you can do.
- **Coffee and non-herbal tea** dehydrate too. You can try to compensate by drinking a glass of water for every cup of coffee or tea you have. Some say this goes for alcohol as well, but that doesn't erase the numbing effect it has.
- **Sodas** can make you burp and cause a bloated feeling that may interfere with your breathing.
- Do you frequently suffer from a dry throat? Try reducing your intake of **salt** (and note that there's salt in more products than you might think).

Drugs and supplements

- **Antihistamine** (used to treat various allergic reactions) is dehydrating, as are certain types of throat lozenges and cough drops.
- Some **other drugs** that may affect the vocal instrument are birth-control pills and various types of hormones and steroids.
- Like alcohol, **recreational drugs** can reduce both your control over, and your awareness of your vocal instrument, apart from having other ill effects — and being illegal.
- You may use additional **supplements** (Echinacea is a very popular one) and vitamins, though a healthy diet can make these supplements less necessary. Some of them may even be counter-effective. For example, **Vitamin C**, which is good for your immune system, can have a dehydrating effect if you use too much of it.
- Nothing beats personal advice in these matters. If you have any questions on what's good for you, please consult a **physician**.

SYMPTOMS AND SOLUTIONS

Some of the symptoms dealt with in the following section stem from common diseases, which to a certain degree can be prevented by a healthy lifestyle. Other symptoms are more specific to singers and others who demand a lot of their vocal instrument. Preventing these symptoms is mostly a matter of using your voice correctly, and trying to avoid overusing it.

Warning signs

The sooner you start with a remedy against any type of disease, the more effective it usually is. Some warning signs for singers? Tiring quickly when singing; a hoarse voice after just one or two songs; a breathy, husky, raspy, gravelly, or hoarse timbre; loss of your highest notes; and a real 'break' rather than an acceptable passaggio.

Classical vs. non-classical

It's probably impossible to say whether classical singers are more at risk than non-classical singers, or vice versa. One clear difference, however, is that classical singers are usually more aware of the warning signs mentioned above. Non-classical singers often don't notice slight changes right away, while classical voices often suffer directly from the subtlest deviations.

Coaching, smoke, and rain

Lack of proper coaching is another reason why non-classical singers may be bothered by vocal problems more often. They're also at higher risk because they often perform in areas where there's a lot of smoke (cigarette smoke in clubs; artificial stage smoke), or on outdoor stages.

Rest

Lots of rest and intensive hydration are two of the most popular and effective remedies against sore, inflamed, irritated, overused, or swollen vocal folds. In some cases, you may even need to refrain from singing (and speaking) for a couple of days, or weeks. Tip: If you're not allowed to speak, do not whisper either; contrary to popular belief, whispering can be harmful to your vocal folds.

Steam

Steaming is a gentle and inexpensive way to help your vocal folds recover, or to clear a stuffed nose and other passages. Pour hot water in a bowl, drape a towel over your head, and breathe in. Keep the water temperature at an agreeable level. If it's too hot, it may do more harm than good. Use plain water only. Adding chamomile to the water is useful when you have a runny nose, but note that chamomile has a dehydrating effect.

Stuffed nose

You can't sing with a stuffed nose. Steaming helps, but a nasal spray is easier and may work faster. If you use a nasal spray for more than three days, the congestion may actually worsen. Two tips: Some nasal sprays are addictive, and some contain antihistamine; both should be avoided. Get up-to-date information from your pharmacist.

Baking soda and salt

You can also dissolve a bit of baking soda and salt (half a teaspoon each) in a cup of warm water, sniff it in through your nose, then let it come out through your mouth. Some medical experts say you only need to do this when you're having symptoms; others say it has a preventive effect too. Consult your physician if you suffer from a chronically blocked nose.

Swollen vocal folds

If you have a URI, be even more careful with your voice than you would otherwise. URIs often cause your vocal folds to swell, which makes them extra vulnerable.

Pneumonia and bronchitis

Coughing is bad for your vocal folds, but in some cases you may just have to: It's the only way to get rid of the mucous from your lungs when your suffering from pneumonia or bronchitis. You can try to cough without closing your glottis, reducing the risk for your vocal folds. This coughing technique sounds somewhat like a hoarse dog barking.

Tickling cough

A cold can make you cough too, and you can be bothered by a tickling cough. In these cases, you may consider using cough-suppressant drugs.

Too much, too thick, or sticky

Your vocal folds are small muscles covered with mucous membrane, and mucous is essential for them to function properly. Problems arise when there's excess mucous, or if the mucous gets too thick and sticky, hindering the vibrations of your vocal folds.

Don't clear it

To get rid of excess mucous, it's very tempting to clear your throat, but you shouldn't. Apart from hurting your vocal folds, it may also have the reverse effect of increasing the production of mucous. What you should do is hum or sing the mucous off of your vocal folds. Sing trills, arpeggios (broken chords), and glissandos, for example, or ask a teacher for suggestions. It takes more time, but it's harmless and it doesn't stimulate mucous production.

Water or nasal spray

You can also sip water or use lemon juice, though the latter can irritate the throat. Some singers use a nasal spray to thin the mucous. Make sure to get a non-addictive spray, without antihistamine. If you think you need medication, consult an ENT-specialist.

No more smoking

When you smoke, extra mucous is produced to reduce the effect of the aggressive smoke. If you stop smoking, the excess production of mucous isn't diminished right away, so you may suffer from superfluous mucous for a few weeks.

Post-nasal drip

If you suffer from sinusitis, your vocal folds can become irritated by mucous that drips down from the infected sinuses. This post-nasal drip can only be remedied by curing the sinusitis.

Hormones

Women can have excess mucous shortly before their period due to hormonal changes. These can also cause hoarseness, and a darker timbre.

Feels like mucous

Swollen vocal folds as a result of gastric reflux can feel like excess mucous. You should treat these symptoms differently, of course. *Refer to page 127 for more information.*

Other diseases

There are many other diseases and conditions that may cause

problems with excess or sticky mucous. Please refer to appropriate sources for more information.

Laryngitis

Various diseases affect the vocal instrument directly. Laryngitis (an infection of the voice box) is one of them. This disease causes your vocal folds to swell and vibrate irregularly, making it impossible to fully close the glottis. As a result, air escapes as you sing or speak. You'll sound hoarse or have a rough voice (dysphonia), and you may even lose your voice temporarily.
The best advice is to stop singing and avoid talking for a couple of days. Steaming helps. If it doesn't, consult a physician.

Hoarseness

Hoarseness or a rough voice can also be the result of a common cold, exposure to smoke, alcohol, or overusing your voice, for example. Rest and hydration will help.

Swellings and scar tissue

Hoarseness can also be caused by local swellings on the vocal folds, such as vocal nodules or polyps (see page 129). Neglected infections or overusing your voice if your vocal folds are swollen or inflamed can produce scar tissue on your vocal folds, which may lead to chronic hoarseness.
Always seek advice if hoarseness doesn't fade in a couple of days, or if it returns very quickly.

Sore throat

A sore, scratchy, dry throat can be soothed by drinking lots of water. Throat lozenges, mints, chewing gum, or hard-boiled sweets can increase saliva production, but that's only a very temporarily relief. You can also enhance saliva production by lightly biting the tip of your tongue, with the added benefit that there's no sugar involved. Menthol lozenges can be harmful as they have a numbing effect, so you can't tell if you're overusing your voice: Pain is a warning sign. Some recommend lemon to soothe the throat, but this can create additional irritation as well.
Others prefer sipping lukewarm (salted) water or herbal tea with honey, either with or without a bit of lemon juice. Note that

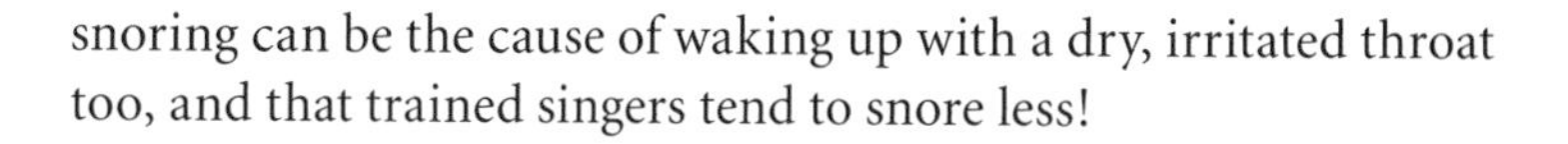

snoring can be the cause of waking up with a dry, irritated throat too, and that trained singers tend to snore less!

Many more

There are many more ways to fight hoarseness, a sore throat, and other symptoms, including yoga, herbal medicine, acupuncture, onions, sea salt, and licorice… Again, please refer to appropriate sources for more information.

Stage fright

Performance nerves are often the main reason for a dry throat — and there's no amount of room temperature water that can fight that dryness. One of the best ways to avoid or reduce stage fright is to prepare yourself well, and make sure you can do it. Know your lyrics, be sure you can sing that one highest note, sing in tune, and don't forget to breathe well. Additionally, there are all kinds of relaxation exercises you can try. Using drugs to fight performance nerves is not a good idea: They have a numbing effect and may reduce your ability to sing well along with your anxiety.

Tonsillitis

Tonsillitis can be a major problem for singers. If it's recurrent, you may consider tonsillectomy. While some experts say that tonsillectomy doesn't influence the voice at all, other experts state that scar tissue can cause a change of timbre, for example. Be sure to tell your doctor you're a singer. This may influence his or her advice.

Acid reflux

Persistent coughing or hoarseness, the sensation of excess mucous on the vocal folds, inflamed vocal folds, and chronic laryngitis are often the result of what's commonly known as acid reflux: Part of the stomach content, including the stomach acid, travels up your esophagus. This irritates the larynx and the vocal folds, with one or more of the above symptoms as a result.

GER(D)

Acid reflux is also known as gastro-esophageal reflux (GER or GERD; the extra D stands for 'disease'). The words gastro and esophageal refer to your stomach and your esophagus, respectively. GERD is caused by an insufficient closure of the stomach opening (e.g., a hiatus hernia).

Burning

Millions of people know what acid reflux can feel and taste like: a burning sensation in the chest, known as heartburn or pyrosis, and a sharp, acid taste in the back of your mouth. Others have acid reflux without these sensations, or it happens as they sleep, without them being aware of it.

Not what you think

Many singers try to fight these symptoms with the wrong means because they think they have excess mucous, while in fact they suffer from acid reflux, which makes their vocal folds feel as if there's excess mucous. If you're not sure what's bothering you, consult your physician. Acid reflux is a very common disease, and antireflux medications are among the world's most prescribed drugs.

Raise your head

You can also try to reduce reflux by raising the head end of your bed some six to eight inches. As an alternative, special GERD-pillows are available. It also helps to avoid food and drinks that stimulate the production of stomach acid, such as coffee, tea, alcohol, and spicy food — and do not eat two to three hours before going to bed.

Vocal nodules, polyps, and cysts

Vocal nodules, polyps, and cysts are different types of growths in or on the vocal folds. Without going too deep into the subject (there are other books that do, yet proper diagnosis and treatment are best left to an ENT-specialist), here are the differences between them, and what can be done about them.

Symptoms

You can't examine yourself for these growths, since you can't see your vocal folds. Instead, visit a doctor if you suffer from a rough, hoarse voice that doesn't go away in a couple of days, if you have a loss of range, if your speaking voice goes down in pitch, or if you have unstable pitch, voice fatigue, or voice loss. Often, the sooner a symptom is discovered, the easier it is to get rid of.

Nodules or nodes

Vocal fold nodules or nodes can be compared to calluses, usually appearing as a result of friction because of an incomplete closure of the glottis: Singing with a hoarse voice can produce nodules. Forcing your voice to do things it can't, and providing inadequate breath support (causing 'wild' air to escape through the glottis) are other potential causes. You can get nodules after just one night of overusing your voice! Nodules always develop in pairs, one on each fold. Women are more at risk than men (they sing and talk about an octave higher, so their vocal folds vibrate twice as fast); boys and girls have the same risk.

Soft to hard

Vocal nodules can come and go unnoticed, but they can cause severe problems too. Initially, nodules are soft. Giving your voice sufficient rest between performances can be enough to make them go away. If they don't fade, they will eventually develop into horny tissue.

Rest or surgery

As long as nodules are soft, vocal rest is the best remedy. Hardened nodules may need to be surgically removed. Speech therapy can help you prevent nodules from returning. Preferably start this therapy before surgery takes place. If surgery is performed well, it shouldn't affect your timbre — but even then, it's better to prevent the nodules from growing rather than have them removed later.

Polyps

A polyp is an enlarged area on one or both vocal folds. Causes for polyps include overusing or misusing the voice, acid reflux, and smoking. Polyps and other growths disturb the even vibration of the vocal folds: That's what changes the quality of your voice.

If your voice sounds rough when singing or speaking softly, and becomes clear when you increase your loudness, chances are you have a polyp. Voice therapy may help, but surgery will often be required.

Cyst

A vocal fold cyst is a small, fluid-containing sac in the vocal fold. That's what makes cysts both harder to spot and harder to remove. Cysts are rare, compared to nodules and polyps.

WHERE TO GO?

A general practitioner is often the best place to start if you suffer from any of the above and need to do something about it. He or she can refer you to a specialist doctor.
For a proper (e.g., stroboscopic) examination of your vocal folds you'll have to see an ENT-specialist, who may in turn refer you to a speech therapist or a speech pathologist. You can go to them directly too, of course, but these specialists may require that you visit a medical doctor first so potential physical problems can be diagnosed.

Speech pathologists and therapists

The difference between a speech therapist and a speech-language pathologist isn't always very clear — it may even depend on the state or the country you're in whether there is a difference — and sometimes there's none, the terms being used interchangeably. If there is a difference between the two professions, it's usually that speech therapists have a bachelor's degree in speech therapy and work in schools only; a speech language pathologist (SLP) has a master's degree in speech language pathology, and can practice both privately and within various organizations. Both specialists treat a large array of speech, language, and communication problems.

Vocologists

Vocology is a young profession, focusing on voice habilitation (rather than just rehabilitation). Practitioners are specialized speech language therapists, ENT-specialists, teachers or trainers, or other vocal experts.

Treating vocalists

Whenever you need help from any of these experts, preferably find one that's used to working with vocalists. Some specialize in treating singers — and some even sing themselves.

Posture, breathing

GPs and other experts can also refer you to other specialists, trainers, or coaches: a physical therapist to improve your posture, for example, or a yoga teacher to work on your breathing or to help you relax, or an allergist.

9

Lyrics

For most singers, lyrics are an essential part of performance. This chapter features some helpful hints on conveying the message of a song, on memorizing lyrics, and on pronunciation.

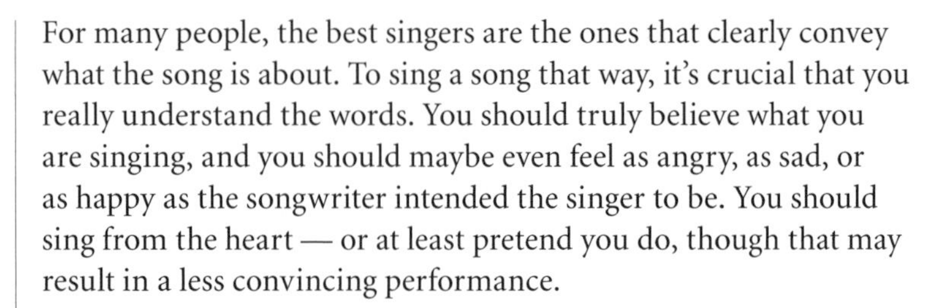

For many people, the best singers are the ones that clearly convey what the song is about. To sing a song that way, it's crucial that you really understand the words. You should truly believe what you are singing, and you should maybe even feel as angry, as sad, or as happy as the songwriter intended the singer to be. You should sing from the heart — or at least pretend you do, though that may result in a less convincing performance.

Automatically

If you really know what you're singing about, you will probably adapt your articulation and timbre to the song automatically, as well as the way you move, the way you look, or any other aspect of your performance.

Your own lyrics

If you write your own lyrics, choose words you believe in. Choose words that convey what you're singing about. Good lyrics show whether you're happy, sad, or angry. Words can be funny or ironic, aggressive or comforting — even on a lyric sheet. Poems do it that way all the time, after all.

Telephone directory

If you haven't got a clue what you're singing about, you might as well replace the original lyric sheets with the first page of a telephone directory. That said, there are singers who can sing names and numbers in a very moving way too, probably by imagining a story or a song that matches the required mood…

The lyrics

The better you understand what the song is about, the easier it is to get its message across, and the easier it will probably be to memorize the lyrics. It can be helpful, for example, to rephrase the story of the song in your own words, line by line, verse by verse, or summarizing the entire song in a few words.

Your musicians

Who should you tell the story to? The musicians in your band! They may have no idea what you are singing about. When they do, they will probably help you to convey the words rather than just accompany them.

Where to get lyrics

You can find the lyrics to the songs you want to sing in CD booklets, of course; there are song books with both lyrics and music for sale; and you can find the lyrics to thousands of popular songs on the Internet (see pages 217–218). If you're not successful that way, you can also copy the words from the CD or the cassette, or another source.

> **Really listen**
>
> *Copying lyrics that way is not as inefficient as it may seem. First, it forces you to really listen and think about the words. Second, writing the words down is actually a great way to help you memorize them.*

Slow them down

Copying the lyrics from a CD or cassette is often easier if you can slow the music down a bit. Some cassette players have this option, but using it lowers the pitch of the song as well. If you have to do this often, you may want to invest in audio editing software that allows you to slow down a song without affecting pitch. This type of software isn't that expensive anymore — and you can use it for a whole lot of other purposes too: Combined with a proper sound card, it turns your computer into a basic home studio.

Aloud

Another way to memorize the lyrics is to read the text aloud, as if you were reading a book, or to declaim it as if you were an actor in a play. Some like to read the lyrics aloud while stretching all the vowels, or to add just the rhythm of the song. You can also sing the song at a single pitch, a bit higher than your speaking pitch, or sing it really, really slow.

Melody

If you want to focus on the melody, simply replace the lyrics by vowels or nonsense syllables (la, la, la, do, dah, do, dah…). This is also helpful for planning your breaths.

PRONUNCIATION

Pronunciation is how you make words sound. This is of course closely related to articulation and diction (see page 74).

Where you're from

The way people pronounce words often tells you where they're from. Texans, New Yorkers, Canadians, Brits, and Australians all speak English, yet they all sound different. And the same goes for Italians, Chinese, or Russians: When they speak English, they all sound different.

Same instrument

People from different backgrounds have different pronunciation not because they have different vocal instruments, but because of the pronunciation of their parents, their siblings, their peers, and other people they grew up with: You learn the language by hearing it.

Accent or suppress

In some styles of music, it may be welcome to stress a certain dialect, or a certain way to pronounce words — after all, country singers are supposed to sound very different from rappers. In other styles, you may have to suppress or adapt the dialect or pronunciation that feels natural to you. Your pronunciation can seriously reduce the power of the song you're singing — because it's way too 'civilized' for one style of music, or too 'uncivilized' for another.

Teachers and pathologists

Teachers can be of great help in learning proper pronunciation and articulation. If you have real problems pronouncing certain words or syllables you may want to consult a speech therapist or speech-language pathologist to (see page 130).

Foreign languages

If you sing in a language that's not your own, pronunciation is of special importance, especially if you sing to an audience that happens to speak that language. Some languages seem impossible to sing in, because of certain sounds they require — Dutch, for example, because of the famous guttural *g* in *Schiphol* or *Scheveningen*. Or other European languages for the *u* in *müde* (tired; German), *muur* (wall; Dutch), or *mûr* (ripe; French); note the three different spellings for three identical sounds! The two wide open *a*'s in the German word *Aria* are just as hard — and those are just a few examples.

Lots of work

You can learn how to pronounce foreign words properly, but it may take a lot of work. Again, not because your vocal instrument is different, but because it's not used to producing those sounds.

Bed or bet

There's one more thing that can make pronouncing words in foreign languages difficult: It may very well be that you just don't hear the subtleties in a particular language. For example, some foreign languages make no difference in the pronunciation of the words 'bed' and 'bet.' If, as a foreign singer, you don't know that difference, you may be unable to hear it — which makes it impossible to pronounce it. The same goes for the subtle difference between 'bad' and 'bed'.

(H)elp

Likewise, French people often have a hard time learning the difference between 'itch' and 'hitch', simply because they're not used to pronouncing an 'h' at the beginning of a word.

Live there

The best way to learn proper pronunciation of a foreign language is of course to learn how to speak it, and preferably even live in

Pot, caught, court

Even native-English speakers aren't always able to hear — and produce — all the subtleties of their own language. For example, the difference between the vowel sounds in 'pot,' 'caught,' and 'court,' is hardly heard, if at all, in certain American dialects, yet it is quite clear in others.

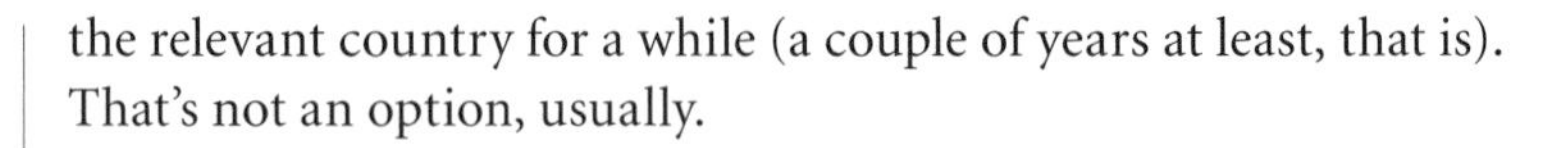

the relevant country for a while (a couple of years at least, that is). That's not an option, usually.

International Phonetic Alphabet

You can also write out the text of the songs you want to sing using the International Phonetic Alphabet (IPA). This alphabet has symbols for all consonant and vowel sounds in English and foreign languages. Learning this alphabet takes time, though: It has more than a hundred symbols.

Regular alphabet

That's why there are many singers who use their own phonetic symbols and the regular alphabet to roughly indicate what words should sound like. For example, the sound of the *j* in the German word *Jahre* is similar to the English *y* in *year*, and to the double *l* in *caballero.*

A few examples from the International Phonetic Alphabet. Not all sounds are used in all languages – and those are often the hard ones to master.

IPA	English	German	French
ə	m**e**lon	irr**e**n (to stray)	ell**e** (she)
ʃ	**sh**ip	**sp**aren (to save)	**ch**anson (song)
ɔ	m**a**ll	d**o**ch	il d**o**rt (he sleeps)
θ	**th**rough	–	–
ɥ	–	–	S**ui**sse (Swiss)

Teacher

To use phonetic notation (either the official alphabet or your own), you need to know how to pronounce the words in the first place. Listening carefully to the songs you intend to sing is one way. Visiting a teacher who has really mastered the language is another.

10

Microphones and Effects

If you go out to buy a microphone, you'll have to choose between dynamic and condenser models, cardioid and other pickup patterns, hi-Z and low-Z mics. This chapter explains all those differences without getting too technical, and advises on what to listen for when comparing microphones. A short section on effect equipment for vocalists is also included.

One good reason to buy your own microphone is that you'll have one that makes you sound as good as possible. Another one is that it's more hygienic: You avoid sharing mics with so-called microphone-kissers — which is very much like sharing gum.

Not a whole lot

For most singers, a microphone is the only piece of equipment they'll ever buy. You don't need to spend a whole lot of money on one: Many pros use microphones that cost no more than one or two hundred dollars.

Cheap

There are plenty of cheaper microphones around. If you really want to save money, at least do yourself the favor of listening to a couple of more expensive models too — if only so you know what you would be missing.

Sound system

If you sing in a band, you'll often use the band's sound system or PA, or the sound system of the venue where you're playing. Even the very best sound system won't do you much good if you don't have the microphone that's best for your voice.

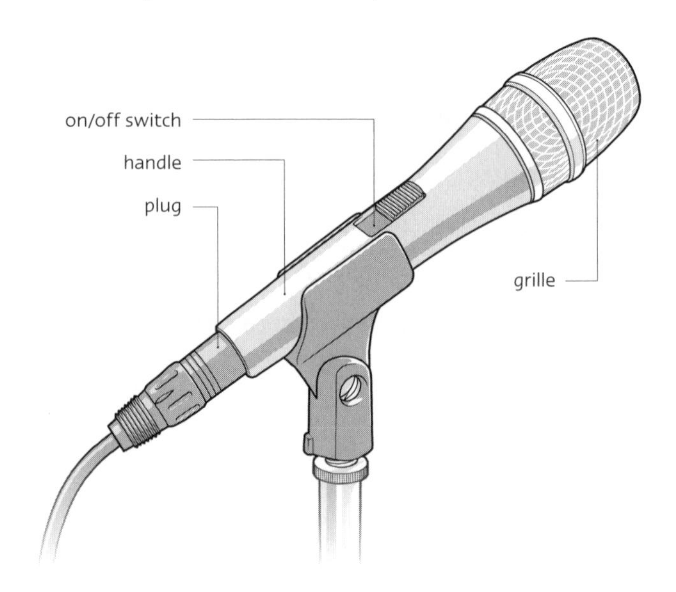

A vocal microphone. (Sennheiser)

Compare models

You can of course simply buy that one, hugely popular microphone that is being used by thousands of singers around the world. But you may be better off with another microphone made by that same company or any of its competitors. Comparing various models can really be worthwhile.

Drum, guitar or vocal

Microphones can be grouped in different ways. First of all, there are microphones for different applications — bass drums, horns, guitar, and so on. Vocal microphones are specifically designed for vocals, but they work great for other instruments as well, even if they're marketed as 'vocal microphones' or 'vocalist microphones' exclusively.

Dynamic or condenser

Second, there are *dynamic* microphones and *condenser microphones.* Their differences are covered below.

Pickup patterns

Third, it's important that a microphone picks up just your voice and nothing else. For that purpose, microphones come with different pickup patterns or sensitivity fields. The type of pattern tells you the angles at which a microphone does and doesn't pick up sound. There's more on this on pages 144–146.

TIP

Handheld or headworn

Most singers use a handheld microphone. Dancing singers and singers/instrumentalists are often better off with a headworn microphone, as described on pages 149–150.

DYNAMIC OR CONDENSER

Historically, dynamic and condenser microphones have many differences. Most singers use a dynamic microphone onstage because dynamic mics are known to be rugged and reliable. Condenser microphones, being more sensitive in many ways, are the most popular choice in studios. Onstage, they're mainly preferred by vocalists who need the expressiveness and subtlety of a condenser, rather than the ruggedness of a dynamic mic. The differences between the two types are fading, however, to some extent. But first, four paragraphs of technical stuff. Skip them if you like.

The difference

Dynamic and condenser microphones can look exactly alike. Their main difference is under the microphone's grille.

Dynamic: coil

A dynamic microphone has a small coil, mounted on a thin diaphragm. When you sing, the vibrating air of your voice makes the diaphragm and thus the coil move in a magnetic field. This movement creates electric signals, which travel to the amplifier through the mic cable.

Condenser: two plates

A condenser microphone has two extremely thin plates: the diaphragm and the backplate. They're both electrically charged. When you sing, the diaphragm moves, which varies the spacing between the two plates. This generates electric signals, which are sent to the amplifier.

Faster

The moving coil in a dynamic microphone is very small. Compared to the diaphragm in a condenser microphone, though, it's quite bulky. The ultra-thin diaphragm can stop and start moving much faster, allowing it to respond to the subtlest nuances in your voice.

Crisp, clear, and direct

The faster response of a condenser translates into a more precise, clear, direct, crisp sound. A condenser is also more sensitive, with enhanced detail and transparency. The response of a condenser mic tends to be more uniform too, bringing out the real timbre of the voice rather than coloring it.

Warm, mellow, and smooth

Conversely, dynamic microphones usually make for a warmer, mellower, more rounded, fatter, fuller, or smoother sound. This is exactly what many rock and other 'popular' singers want, both live and in the studio. Dynamic mics typically can handle higher sound pressure levels (SPL) too.

Microphone distance

A major difference between dynamic and condenser microphones is how they respond to the distance between your mouth and the microphone. With a condenser microphone you can vary the distance quite a lot, using it as an extra means to adjust your vocal color and to enhance the dynamics of your performance. This requires good microphone technique. What you get in return is more expressiveness.

Too far

A dynamic microphone offers less possibilities for variation: If you hold it even slightly too far away the sound gets very thin. Move it a bit further, and no one will be able to hear you anymore. Singing very close to a microphone has the same effect with both dynamic and condenser mics (proximity effect; see page 157).

Fading differences

Some of the differences between dynamic and condenser mics are fading. Traditionally, condenser microphones were more sensitive to handling noise and *feedback* (the loud *skreee* you hear if a microphone picks up sound from a loudspeaker and feeds it back to the amplifier, from where it's sent to the loudspeaker again — and so on…).

Just as good

Modern condensers, however, can be almost or just as good as dynamic microphones in both respects. Likewise, some modern dynamic microphones can make your voice sound as transparent and clear as a condenser would.

Affordable models

Condenser microphones used to be much more expensive, but

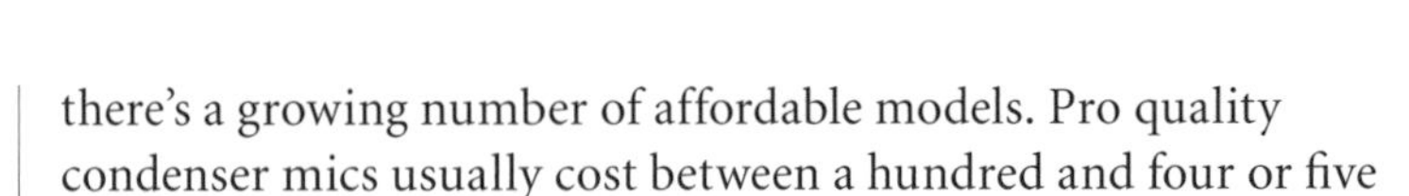

there's a growing number of affordable models. Pro quality condenser mics usually cost between a hundred and four or five hundred dollars.

Power

There's one more technical difference between condenser and dynamic models: Condenser microphones need to be powered. Usually, this power is supplied by the sound system through the mic's cable, either directly from the (powered) mixer or from a separate power unit. This is known as *phantom power*, because there is no separate cable supplying power to the mic.

Batteries

Some condenser mics can run on batteries too, either to take over should phantom power fail, or to be used instead of phantom power. Batteries are more expensive and less reliable, however.

PICKUP PATTERN

The pickup pattern or sensitivity field of a microphone indicates how it reacts to sound coming from different directions. It's also known as the microphone's *polar pattern*, *response pattern*, or *directivity response.*

Omnidirectional

Some types of microphones are designed to pick up sound from all directions. You'll hardly ever find these *omnidirectional microphones* onstage, as they very easily pick up the sound from monitors and other speakers, thus creating feedback.

Unidirectional

You're usually better off with a *unidirectional microphone*, which picks up sound from one (*uni*) direction only. Unidirectional microphones are available with pickup patterns in different 'shapes.' The three main types of pickup patterns are known as *cardioid*, *supercardioid*, and *hypercardioid*.

Heart-shaped: cardioid

Many popular microphones have a heart-shaped or *cardioid* pickup pattern. As you can see below, these microphones reject sound that comes from the rear, where a single monitor would be. Sound that comes off-axes is reduced.

Cardioid and supercardioid microphones reject sound from various angles. An omnidirectional microphone picks up sound from all angles.

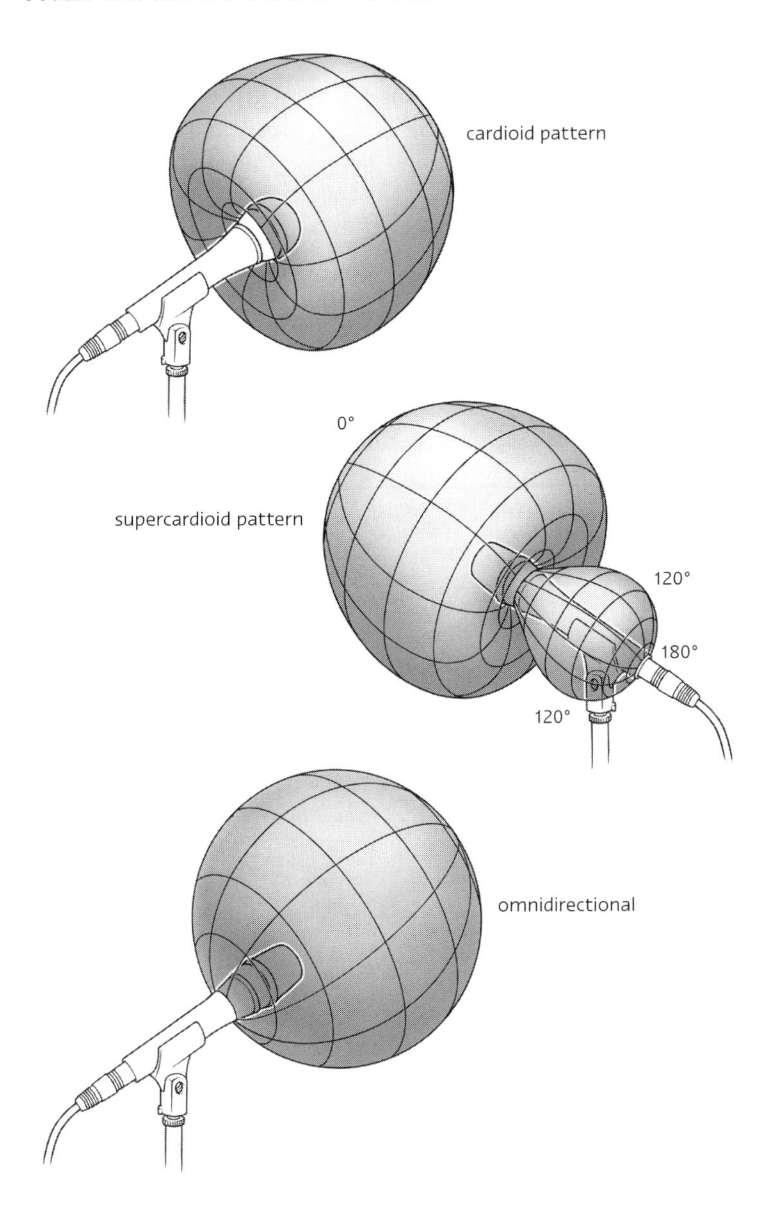

Supercardioid

The next popular variation is the *supercardioid*, which has a tighter heart-shaped pattern. It is focused on the front (at 0°), with a bit of sensitivity on the rear (at 180°), and it's most insensitive around 120°. This is very effective on stages with a PA system.

Hypercardioid

On very loud stages, you may be better off with a microphone that has a *hypercardioid* pickup pattern. A hypercardioid has an even tighter pickup angle at the front.

Cardioid, super, differoid

Most microphones have either a cardioid or a supercardioid pattern. These are not the only variations on the theme; for example, there are mics with *differoid* pickup patterns too.

Switchable

Some (condenser) mics, mostly studio models, have two or more polar patterns that can be selected with a switch. Other designs allow you to change the polar pattern with a separate cap — but these are quite rare.

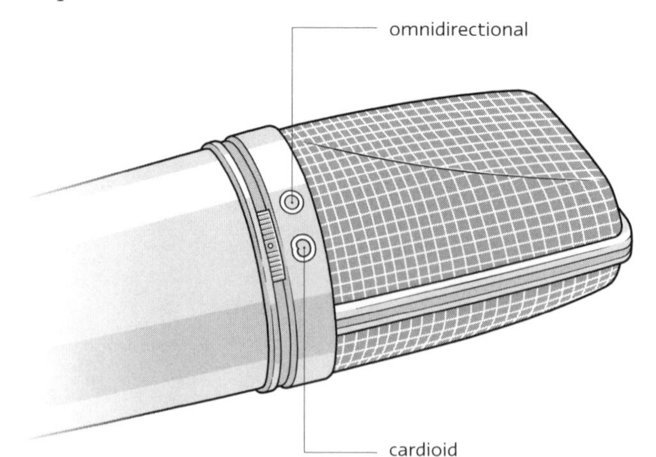

... A choice between omnidirectional and cardioid patterns on a studio microphone.

More patterns

Omnidirectional microphones and microphones with other pickup patterns (*e.g., Figure-8*) are mostly used in studios.

WIRELESS

A wireless microphone buys you a lot of extra freedom to move around onstage. Wireless mics cost a lot more, and they may not sound exactly the same as their wired counterparts.

Transmitter

Many microphones are available in wired and wireless versions. The wireless version has a transmitter built into the microphone,

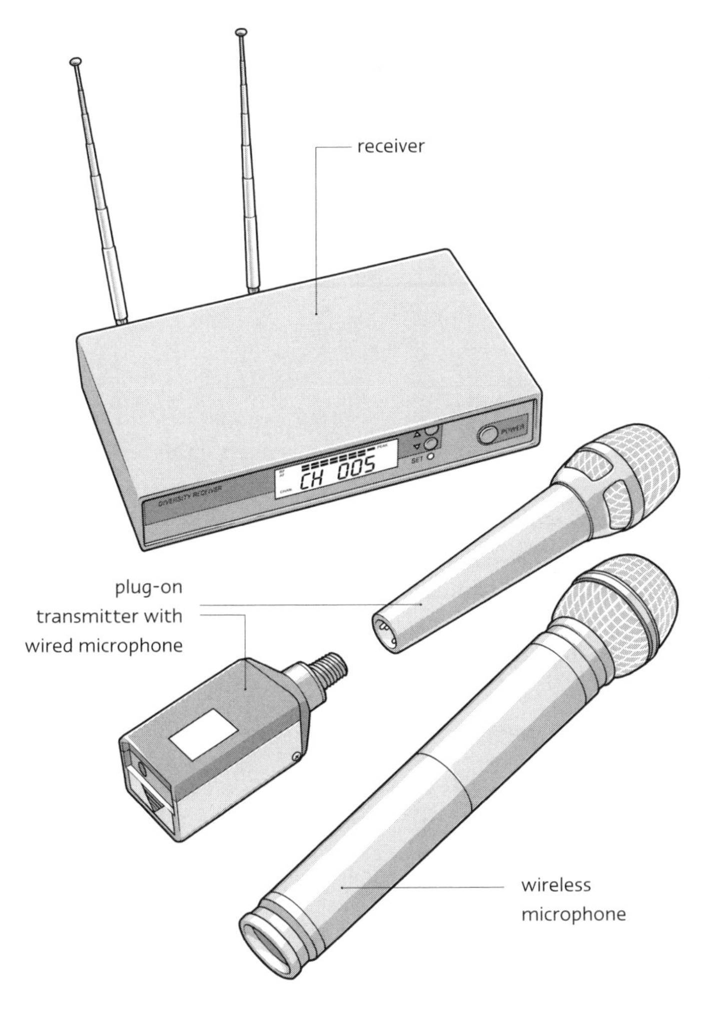

A wireless microphone, a microphone with plug-on transmitter, and a receiver.

which makes it a bit more bulky. The transmitter sends the electric signals to a receiver. The receiver is connected to the amp or the mixing board.

The same?

Do wireless and wired microphones sound the same? Opinions differ. You may have a better sound, less noise, and more reliability if you compare a regular cable to an affordable transmitter and receiver — but not always. If you buy professional gear, which easily costs four or five times as much, the differences will be negligible. Great artists wouldn't use wireless mics if they weren't good.

Plug-on

If you have a microphone you like, you can also buy a plug-on transmitter and a receiver. That means that you don't have to get used to another (bigger) microphone, and it's often cheaper than buying a complete wireless system. Performance quality may decline, however, or the sound may change, for better or worse. The transmitter also increases the weight and alters the balance of your mic.

Frequency range

Wireless systems use different frequency ranges to send the signals from the mic to the receiver. Most systems use either *VHF* or *UHF*.

The difference

UHF-systems typically cost more, but they're less sensitive to interference, the maximum distance between mic and receiver can be much bigger, power output is higher, and the transmitter's batteries last longer — say, twelve hours and up, rather than some eight to twelve hours.

Prices

Compared to an identical wired microphone, a complete, professional quality wireless system typically costs six to ten times as much.

HEADSETS

If you play an instrument while singing, you may consider buying a headworn microphone, also known as a headset. A *wireless headset* is a great solution for singers who also dance or move around a lot onstage.

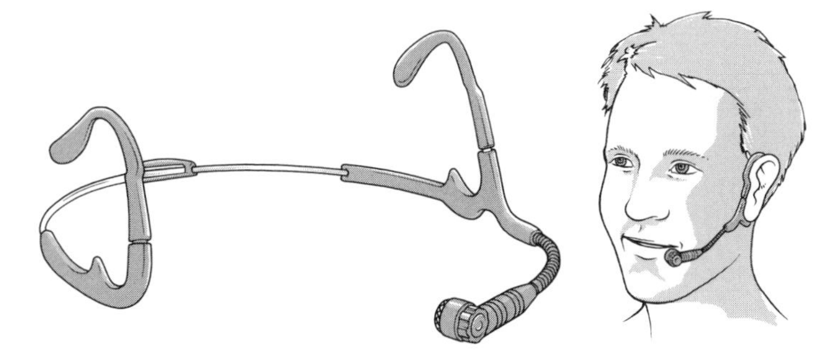

A headset.

Condenser and beltpack

Headsets have miniature condenser mics; the electronics are in a small *beltpack* or *bodypack* that you clip onto your belt. The headset frames are often fully adjustable for a perfect fit. To allow you to communicate with your fellow musicians without the audience hearing you, the mic can often be moved aside.

Switches

Some mics have an on/off switch, which should be absolutely noiseless. Another switch that you may come across allows you to adjust the mic's sensitivity to the loudness of your voice.

Your hands

A headset doesn't allow for variations in timbre or dynamics by changing the distance between your mouth and the mic — and in some cases, not having a microphone to hold onto can make you wonder what to do with your hands...

Prices

Prices of headsets tend to be slightly higher than what you'd pay for a regular mic of similar quality.

Even smaller

Broadway musical singers and other vocalists often use extremely small, (almost) invisible wireless microphones, which can be attached to a pair of glasses, for example, or glued to your head, very close to the hairline, covered by a wig or your own hair. These microphones are very expensive.

FEATURES

Here are some of the main features microphones have — or don't have.

Cable

Cheap mics often have a permanently-attached cable. This makes your mic quite vulnerable, as the cable and its plug, and the attachment to the microphone, usually are the weakest points. Another piece of advice: If you get yourself a microphone with a detachable cable, buy a spare cable right away.

XLR

Mics with a detachable cable usually have a three-pin connector,

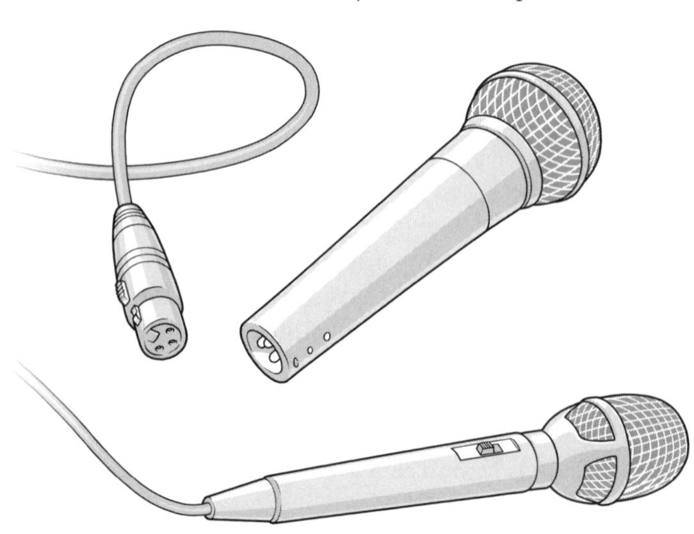

A professional microphone with a three-pin XLR or Canon connector, and a budget microphone with a permanently attached cable and a 1/4" phone plug.

known as an XLR or Canon-style connector. At the other end, the cable usually enters a similar input on the mixing board or the amp.

(Un)balanced

XLR-connections are usually *balanced*. They're less sensitive to noise and hum than ¼" phone plug connections, which are typically *unbalanced*.

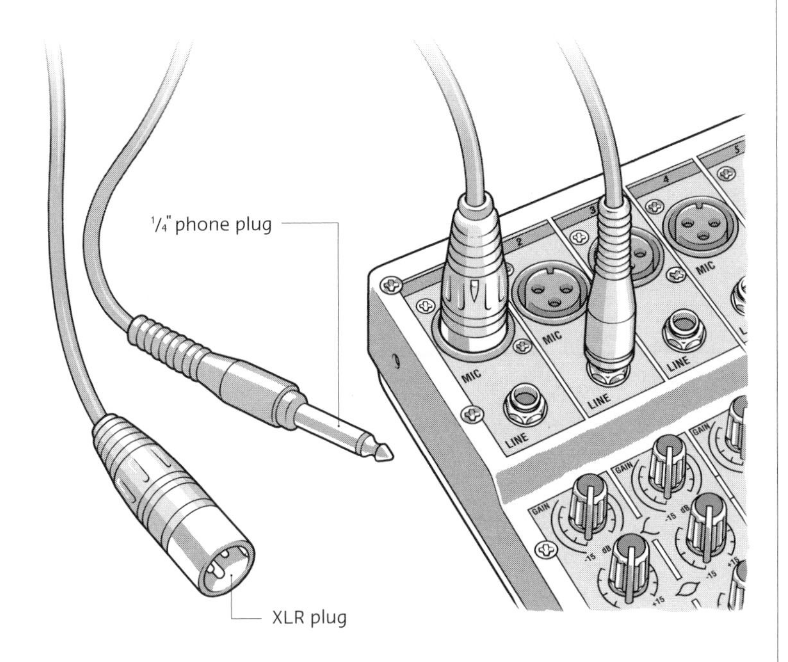

Balanced XLR (above) and unbalanced ¼" phone inputs (below) on a basic mixing board.

Low Z

Cheap mics with ¼" phone plugs are usually *high-impedance* or *high Z mics*. Without getting into technical details, this means that using long cables will reduce the mic's high-frequency response. Mics with an XLR-style connection are low-impedance or low-Z mics; cables of ten meters (30 ft) or more are no problem.

On/off

Quite a few microphones have an on/off switch; on some models it's an option. If there is one, it should be noiseless. On/off switches can be very practical, but they can also be off when you hope they're on — or vice versa, which may be even more painful. On some mics, the switch can be locked, and it's often designed so that you can't turn it on or off inadvertently.

Low-cut

The closer you get to a microphone, the bassier the sound gets (see page 157). Some microphones have a *low-cut* or *bass roll-off* switch to reduce this so-called proximity effect. Another switch, allowing you to choose between two or more polar patterns, was mentioned earlier in this chapter.

Accessories

Some microphones come with a matching holder to mount the mic on a stand. The thread of the holder may be different from the microphone stand's thread. This problem is solved with a 3/8" > 5/8" (or vice versa) *thread adaptor.*

Various microphone clamps and thread adaptors.

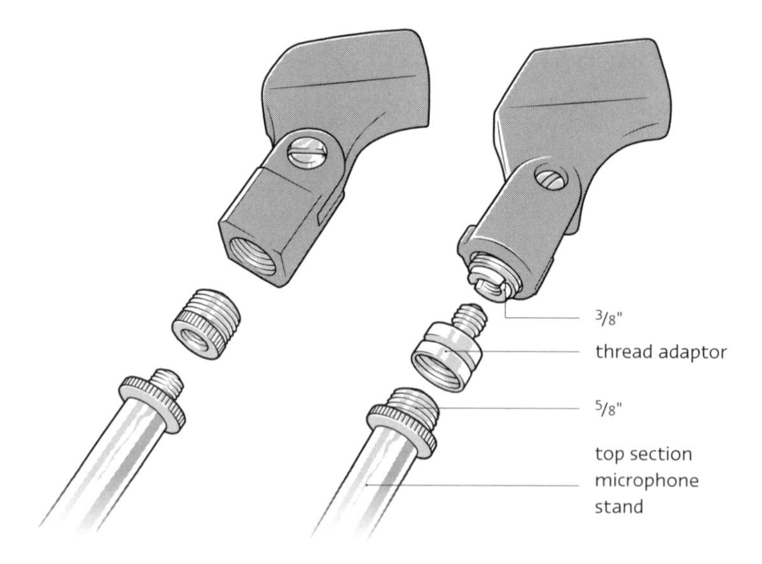

Case

A good case with a shock-absorbing lining definitely extends your mic's life expectancy. A microphone pouch usually offers less protection.

Pop filter

Most vocal microphones have a built-in filter to reduce *pops*: the 'explosions' you create when singing plosive consonants (*e.g.*, P, B, T). A built-in *pop filter* usually consists of a thin ply of special foam that covers the inside of the grille.

A large-membrane studio microphone with a pop filter.

Reducing noise

You can also use a thicker foam cover that fits over the grille. These covers can help reduce pop sounds, as well as wind noise when singing outdoors — which explains why they're also known as *windshields.* A windshield also reduces the sibilant noise of consonants that produce a lot of air flow (S, T, CH, SH, etc.), and it protects the microphone against moisture from your breath. Brightness, transparency, or clarity may be reduced, however. Windshields are available in various colors.

Studio pop filter

In studios, a pop filter or *popper stopper* is either a foam disc or a type of fabric mounted in a round frame, put in front of the microphone. They're *acoustically transparent* (they let sound

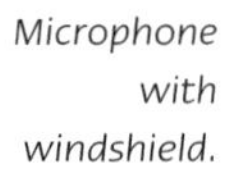

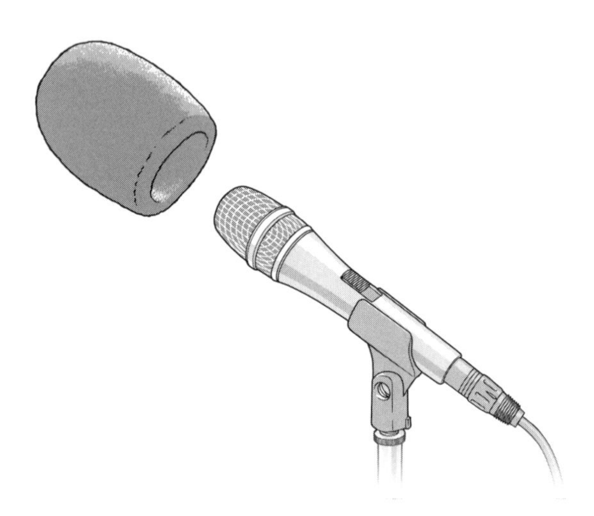

Microphone with windshield.

pass), but they reduce the explosive bursts of air created by P's and other plosives (see page 77).

Singing off-axis

Another way to avoid or reduce pops is to hold the microphone not directly in front of your mouth, but slightly off-axis, or to sing slightly over the microphone.

A GOOD MICROPHONE

In the end, buying a microphone is mostly a matter of using your ears, trying to find the mic that makes your voice sound best. Of course, to make the right decision, you have to know what to listen for.

Read and try

To find a good microphone, you can just go into a store and ask for help, armed with the information above. If you want to prepare yourself even better, get hold of microphone brochures, read microphone reviews in musicians' magazines and on the Internet, and visit the websites of mic manufacturers. Above all, try a few microphones before you decide to buy one. A good salesperson can help you to make a basic selection, based on the style of music you sing, and on your timbre and range.

A few

The best situation to try a microphone is in your band, either in a rehearsal room or live. Not too many stores will lend you a few mics, but you may be able to borrow two or three different microphones from other vocalists. Try them out one after the other, so you can really compare them and focus on their subtle differences.

Recording

If you have to judge mics in a store, see if it's possible to bring a recording of your band, so you can hear your voice in its proper context.

> **Equally loud**
>
> *When trying mics out, either live or in a store, it's best to hook them all up in a mixer, and adjust them so they're all equally loud. Don't use any EQ (bass, treble, and mid in neutral positions), reverb, or any other effects. Just sing, and listen carefully. To really judge the sound, rather than prices, looks, or brand names, keep your eyes closed and ask someone else to hand you the microphones one by one.*

Two or three

If you listen to too many mics in a row, you'll get confused. Try two or three; replace the one you like least for another mic, and so on. Don't go on for too long, but take a break after ten or fifteen minutes. If you already have a microphone and you want to replace it with a better one, bring it along: Your own microphone is a great reference point.

Everything

Sing high, sing low, sing loudly and softly — sing everything you plan to use the mic for. Your biggest notes shouldn't distort; the softest words should be picked up impeccably and directly. If you get gradually louder, the amplified sound should do so too. Low notes should sound clear and not too bassy, and high notes should have body.

Neutral

Microphones differ in how neutral they are. In most studio situations, mics are supposed to be completely neutral and just pick up what they 'hear.' Onstage however, such a microphone would make you sound shallow. Live mics need to add a little color to your voice.

Frequency response

The way microphones color your voice is one of the main things to listen for: That is the way a mic 'sounds.' This is determined by how it responds to various frequency ranges — in technical terms, by its *frequency response.*

Flat or boosted

A mic that's completely neutral has a *flat* frequency response. Live vocal mics boost certain frequency ranges and cut others a bit. This can make them sound either warmer, more aggressive, brighter, more powerful, smoother, more open, or fat, full, delicate, rich, dry, sizzling, piercing, thin, big, husky, round, gritty, mellow, strident, powerful, brittle, snappy, vibrant, crisp, or dark — just like voices, and just like musical instruments.

High and low

When judging microphones, listen to their overall sound, but also try to distinguish what they do with the lowest and highest frequencies of your voice. Microphones can have a great high end but mushy lows, for example; or warm, full-bodied lows yet brittle, thin highs; or great highs and lows, but mids that are too strong or weak.

Know your voice

The idea is to find a mic whose characteristics can help enhance or compensate for certain characteristics of your voice. If you tend to sound a bit thin, a bright sounding mic will make you sound even thinner — so get one that adds a bit of warmth and body. Conversely, if your natural sound is somewhat subdued, get a mic that adds some clarity to your voice. There are microphones that are great for singers with full voices, and others to enhance young, bright, and clear voices, and so on. The better you can tell a sales person what your voice sounds like, the better he or she will be able to help you.

Mask or reveal

Some microphones make everyone sound good. They usually do so by masking subtle, undesirable nuances. Unfortunately, they also mask the desirable nuances. In other words, these microphones tend to make everyone sound acceptable, but they make no one sound exceptional. The better a singer you are, the more you may want to find a microphone that reveals your qualities, rather than one that masks the subtleties of your voice.

Proximity effect

Unidirectional microphones sound increasingly bassier and warmer as you get closer to them. Many singers use this *proximity effect* to their advantage, with the added warmth and depth flattering their voices. Note that certain microphones can get boomy and muddy when you get too close, while others are designed to sound best when your lips actually touch the grille.

Distances

Microphones also respond differently to moving them away from you. Try each microphone at various distances, and see how playing around with that distance can add to your performance.

Angle

Also vary the angle of the microphone. Mainly focus on what happens in the high frequency range when varying the mic's angle away from the 'standard' position, which is at about 45°.

Pop and sshhh

Some mics may be less sensitive to your plosives (see pages 77 and 153) than others. Likewise, some may be more or less sensitive to your sibilant speech sounds (see page 153).

Most singers hold their microphones at an angle of about 45°.

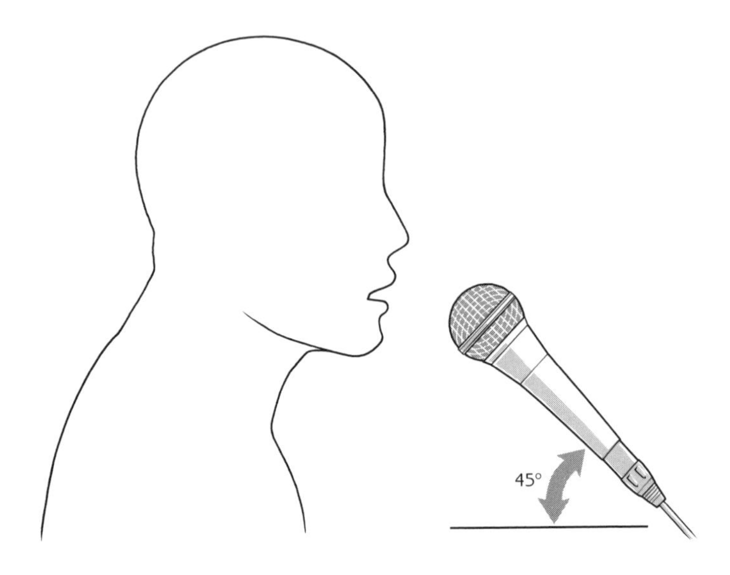

Feedback

Feedback rejection isn't easy to check in a store, but it's good to know that some mics are more sensitive to this gruesome effect than others, independent of their pickup pattern.
If you often sing in a feedback-sensitive environment (a loud band, lots of speakers, small rooms with hard walls), search for a mic that claims to have 'high gain before feedback' or 'great feedback rejection' — though you may not always get what you were promised.

Handling noise

Try mics for handling noise. Internal shock mounts help, and so do rubberized handles, for example.

Feel good

The perfect microphone sounds great, but feels good too. The handle shouldn't be too wide or too narrow for your hands, the balance of the mic should feel comfortable, and the weight should be acceptable. Note that minor differences may become quite substantial after holding a mic for an hour.

Weight

Most popular microphones weigh some 6 to 10 oz (200–350 grams), but don't be surprised to find models that weigh 16 oz or more. Wireless microphones are always bigger and have a different balance because of the built-in transmitter.

Trust your ears

Microphone catalogs often contain more technical data than you can handle. Manufacturers probably put all those numbers in because it's easier to indicate sound in figures and frequency curves than it is to describe it in words. Judging a microphone by its technical data requires a lot of knowledge and experience — so you'd probably better trust your ears.

AND MORE

Some additional information on maintenance, spare parts, brand names, and — once more — feedback.

Grille and pop filter

As you sing with your mouth quite close to the microphone, it's not a bad idea to have it cleaned from time to time. Some singers do this themselves, but taking the grille off isn't always easy, and taking out and properly replacing a built-in pop filter may be very hard. For these and other reasons it's advisable to have your mic cleaned by a technician: Ask your dealer for advice.

Cables and batteries

Microphone cables are vulnerable. Don't stand on them, don't pull them, and always bring a spare one. They're available in various lengths, up to thirty feet (10m) or more. If your mic uses batteries, always bring extras.

Spare mic

Some singers even bring a spare mic. Or they have two different microphones anyway — one for loud, heavy rock songs and one for sensitive ballads, for example. Or mics with different pickup patterns to match conditions in various venues or rehearsal rooms. Or a dynamic mic for live performances and a condenser in the studio. Or a wired one in case your transmitter breaks down, or in case there's too much interference, or...

Studio mics

Want to record your voice for practicing, demos, or other purposes? There's a growing number of affordable studio condenser mics available. Some of these very sensitive, large membrane mics (see illustration on page 153) are available for less than two hundred dollars. Professional studios use similar microphones that cost at least ten times as much.

In-ear monitors

If you predominantly sing amplified, you may want to invest in a pair of in-ear monitors, rather than use traditional monitor speakers. In-ear monitors help prevent feedback, and their sound and volume doesn't change as you move across the stage. Most importantly, they don't have to compete with the sound of the band: They're in your ears, so you can use them at a very moderate volume. This helps prevent hearing loss (they reduce the sound of the band too!), and it helps save your voice as you don't have to strain to sing over the band. That makes singing in tune easier too, and it may very well improve your overall performance. A disadvantage is that they may hinder communication with your fellow band members and your audience. Wireless in-ear monitors are available from around seven or eight hundred dollars.

Microphone brands

Some of the main microphone brands are AKG, Audio-Technica, Audix, Behringer, Beyerdynamic, Crown, Electro Voice, Samson, Sennheiser, and Shure. Some of these companies make low-budget mics only; others have mics in all price ranges. Neumann and Røde specialize in studio microphones.

Never

One more tip on microphone technique: Many musicians and technicians have gone temporarily deaf because of feedback, standing close to a speaker that emits this loud, penetrating sound. If you're the one holding the mic that causes feedback, don't cover it with your hand, but simply point it away from the speaker — and never again hold it so that its sensitive areas are aimed at a speaker.

EFFECTS

The most widely used electronic effect for singers is a *reverb*, which adds a bit of depth to your voice, making it sound less dry. But there are other beneficial effects too. Some singers like to buy their own equipment; others use the band's sound system and effects. Here's some very basic information about equipment that may be useful to you.

Tipcode VOCALS-021

This Tipcode gives some insight in what electronic effects can do.

Reverb

Most reverb units or built-in reverbs are digital devices that allow for a variety of adjustments. You can often select an acoustic model based on the type of room (a church has a different reverb than a hall or a stadium, for example), and you can adjust the length of the reverb and the *pre-delay* (how long it takes before you hear the reverb).

Compressor

Lyrics get easily lost when you sing too loudly or too softly. A *compressor* can help to even out your volume level. It boosts your voice when it's too soft, and reduces the signal when you sing too loud.

Other effects

There are many other effects that can help enhance your performance. Some examples? A *delay* can double your voice, adding a little body to it. An *exciter* adds a lively sparkle to your sound. A *de-esser* reduces sibilant sounds (see page 153). You want some backing vocals but you're all by yourself? Then there are products that multiply your voice, creating additional harmonies as you sing.

Guitarist's effects

Some vocalists like to experiment with effects that are used mainly by guitarists, such as a *distortion*, a *flanger*, a *wah-wah*, or a *chorus*. These are usually used to alter the sound of the voice, rather than to enhance it.

Singer's workstations

Various companies make special effect equipment for vocalists, *e.g.*, vocalist workstations or vocal effect processors. They often include some of the effects mentioned above, as well as other effects and features.

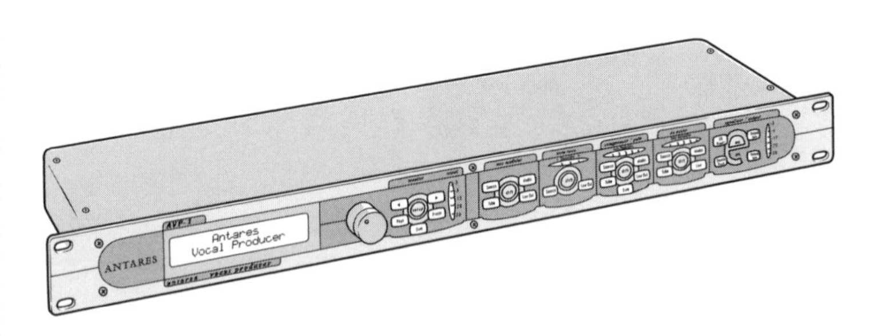

... special equipment for singers, featuring pitch correction, microphone modeling, a compressor, a de-esser, and more... (Antares)

Pitch correction

Some special features are *pitch correction* (corrects your pitch in real time, as you sing!) and *microphone modeling* (offers you a variety of virtual microphone models).

Amplifiers, sound systems, and effects

Should you consider buying your own amplifier or sound

Tipcode VOCALS-022
The effects of electronic pitch correction: what it sounds like, and what it should sound like!

system, or would like to know more about effects? Check out *Tipbook Amplifiers & Effects* (see page 227). This book also offers additional technical information on microphones.

11

History

The voice is the world's oldest instrument. This chapter highlights just a few of the main points of a history that will largely remain unrevealed.

Nothing is really certain when it comes to the early history of the singing voice, and there's a lot of debate on how and when things evolved in more recent times.

Safe guess

It's a safe guess that mankind has been singing for hundreds of thousands of years, in daily life, in ceremonies and rituals, and later on, in theatrical settings. It is often assumed that singing as an art form originated from reciting texts, when people realized that adding a melody to their words would enhance and embellish their message.

Gregorian chants

The history of the voice can only be studied in detail from the period that music was written down. Some of the earliest examples of written Western music are the Gregorian chants, dating back some fourteen hundred years.

Monodic

For hundreds of years, the Gregorian chants were *monodic*: There was just a single melody, and nothing else. The singer was known as the *tenor* — he who 'kept' the melody, from the Latin word *tenere*, to keep.

Bassus, altus, superius

Around 1100, a second melodic line was added, lower in pitch, and later on a third line, higher in pitch. The additional singers were referred to as the *counter tenor bassus* and the *counter tenor altus* respectively. (Altus means high, as in 'altitude.') A fourth line, even higher in pitch, was sang by the *superius* or *sopra*.

Voice types

This is where the names of the current voice types originate. Initially, they didn't refer to the *range* of the voice of the singer or his timbre, but to the *role* he was singing.

Polyphony

In the years that followed, polyphony ('many voices') developed even further, and choirs could have as many as eight different voices. It is of course quite possible that polyphony came to existence in other cultures much earlier.

Falsettists and castratos

Originally, the highest parts in Western polyphony were performed by male vocalists singing in their falsetto register. In the sixteenth and seventeenth centuries, these *falsettists* were gradually replaced by *castratos*: male singers that had been 'unmanned,' usually around age nine, thus preserving their boy's voices. Some sources say that the Byzantine (Greece Orthodox) church employed castratos as early as the thirteenth century.

Women?

Why haven't women sung these high parts? Because they were not allowed to sing liturgical chants in the churches. Incidentally, this interdiction was based on a misinterpreted command of Apostle Paul in the New Testament.

Opera

Opera originated in Italy, around 1600, a reaction to the polyphony in which lyrics had become less and less intelligible. From the very start, castratos played a main part in opera. Their range was similar to that of the modern soprano or mezzo-soprano.

Women!

In opera, female vocalists took over from the castratos in the late eighteenth century; women singers had slowly become accepted in secular (non-religious) music from the late seventeenth century onward.

Dark and weighty

For many years, the ideal singer's voice had a light timbre, and volume or projection weren't particularly important. This started to change in the first half of the nineteenth century. Bigger opera houses and bigger orchestras required more volume, and the musical instruments of those days called for darker, weightier vocal timbres — a development that continued well into the twentieth century.

New ways

In the twentieth century, composers and vocalists have begun to explore new ways to use the vocal instrument, finding musical applications for yelling, controlled shouting, chattering, smacking, barking, slurping, moaning, grunting, speech singing, electronic manipulation of the voice, and a multitude of other sounds and effects.

Range, dynamics, timbre

Summing it up, the vocal instrument has enormously expanded over the years. The range of classical singers, traditionally limited to about an octave and a half, gained an octave or more. The dynamic range grew as well, and the number of ways to color the voice and to use the vocal instrument — from Gregorian chant to experimental music — has increased enormously.

Voice and instruments

There has always been a strong relationship between the singing voice and the musical instruments of an era. For example, when Flemish composers started to use lower-sounding voices in their works, some time in the fifteenth century, musicians needed lower-sounding instruments than the violins and violas of that time. Eventually this led to the development of the cello.

Beatles and Stones

In non-classical music, the link between the sound of the band and the sound of the voice has always been at least as strong. The clean sound of a big band in the swing era required another timbre than bebop did in the 1940s. Electric guitars called for yet another style of singing, and the timbre of Paul McCartney's voice definitely fit the Beatles better than the Rolling Stones — just like Mick Jagger would have sounded out of place with the Beatles.

The microphone

Non-classical singers often sounded quite a lot like their classical colleagues until the early years of the twentieth century, when the microphone was introduced. Amplification allowed vocalists to use their entire dynamic range, from a whisper to a yell, and to experiment with coloring the sound of their voices without any need to worry about projection. Likewise, blues shouters didn't need to shout anymore in order to be heard — though this hardly ever changed their way of singing.

Scat, vocalese, rap...

Over the years, vocalists in a wide variety of musical styles have found new ways to use their voices: Louis Armstrong's scat singing in the 1920s (replacing words by nonsense syllables), Eddie Jefferson's *vocalese* in the 1940s (singing lyrics to well-known instrumental jazz solos), the intense speechifying of rap in the late 1970s, the sludgy, rough, screaming, distorted sound of grunge in the 1980s.

Inventions

Two technological inventions have been of major importance to the development of the art of singing. One is the microphone and its related devices. The other is the *laryngoscope*, an instrument that allowed its inventor, the Spanish baritone and teacher Manuel García, to see and research the vocal folds. García's laryngoscope and his famous book *Traité complet de l'art du chant (A Complete Treatise on the Art of Singing)* date back to the 1840s.

Improvements

In the years that followed, many new instruments and methods have been developed to further research the vocal instrument, and many new discoveries have been made as a result of those developments. Yet even now, many questions are still unanswered — but that doesn't stop singers from continuing their efforts to further explore and improve their instrument.

12

Being Prepared

A dry throat, butterflies in your stomach, jitters and shakes, weak knees, trembling fingers, a throbbing heart... All familiar sensations experienced by most anyone who ever climbed a stage to perform, audition, or take a music exam—and those who claim they've never experienced such symptoms are often said to be lying or dead!

Nervousness and performing go hand in hand. It's a sign that you're undergoing an adrenaline rush, and without it, performances may be less exciting for both the musicians and the audience. But stage fright can get so bad that it causes you to fail an audition, not make the grade, or mess up your performance. This chapter shares some ideas on reducing audition anxiety, stage fright, and exam nerves.

Books

Many books have been written on this subject, and there is a whole lot more to be said and taught about it. The tips in this chapter touch the mere basics; and as obvious as they seem, they're often quite effective.

Adults and kids

Kids seem to suffer less from jitters and other anxiety symptoms than most teens and adults. So one of the best ways to prevent such feelings in the first place is to begin performing in public at an early age, be it with a school choir, or singing or playing mini-recitals for the family every now and then — even if it's only briefly. As taking this advice may not be an option if you're already beyond early childhood, keep on reading...

PREPARING YOURSELF

First, a look at what could, or should, be done beforehand.

Practice, practice, practice

If you're not fully prepared for a performance or an audition, you have every reason to be nervous. Practicing efficiently, possibly under the guidance of a teacher, is one key to abating performance anxiety. A tip: The closer the time of the main event comes, the more important it is to focus practice sessions on problem areas, rather than on songs you already know very well. A rule of thumb is to be able to play or sing the tricky bits at least five to ten times in a row without stumbling. Only then can you be sure that you've

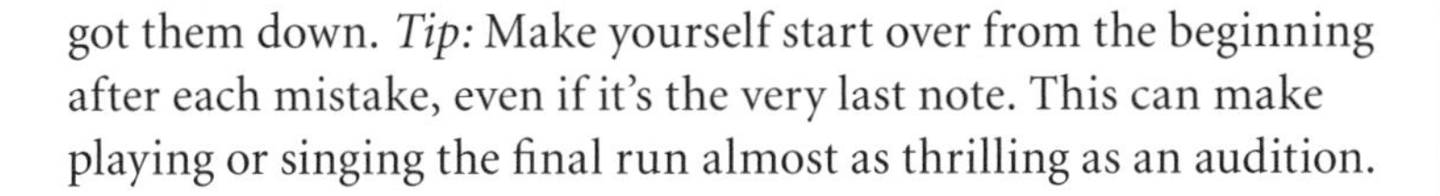

got them down. *Tip:* Make yourself start over from the beginning after each mistake, even if it's the very last note. This can make playing or singing the final run almost as thrilling as an audition.

Slips

Even professionals make mistakes, so preparing a piece includes preparing for stumbles and slips. Practice how to recover quickly and continue to play or sing in the correct tempo. You can learn how to deal with slip-ups. One simple tip: do not make a face as this will just draw everyone's attention to your mistake. Note that there are music teachers who specialize in audition preparation!

Memory

You may sing or play from memory to impress the jury or the members of the band, but consider bringing your sheet music and lyrics along if memorization was not required. Having it there will make it easier to start over if you do slip. Does your piece require page turning? Then it would be helpful to memorize the first section on the following page. Another tip for auditions or exams: Make sure you make a list of the songs you're going to sing or the pieces you're going to play, and don't forget to bring it with you. It really doesn't look good if you've forgotten the title of your next piece.

Accompanist

If you're going to sing with an accompanist, it's best if that's the same person you've rehearsed with. Performing with a stranger can cause added tension, and a familiar face can be a great confidence booster. Even if not required, you may want to consider doing your piece with accompaniment. Having another person there may help reduce stress, and it usually makes for a more entertaining performance too.

Deal with it

No matter how well-prepared you are, auditions and performances will induce stress and nervousness. Dealing with this is part of the learning process of playing or singing, period. Practice doesn't make perfect, but the more you play and perform (and the more auditions etc. you do), the better you will eventually become at handling stage fright.

Surrender

Fighting your nerves is not a good idea either. Doing so can even add to your stress level, which is probably already substantial. Telling yourself to be calm usually doesn't work either. You aren't calm, so it's actually better to just surrender to that. The fact that your nerves can make your performance less than brilliant just shows how important it is to be well-prepared.

Getting used to it

The more used to playing or singing for an audience you are, the less likely you are to be nervous for auditions and similar situations. Still, these situations are different from regular performances: They occur less frequently and there's usually a lot riding on them. A mistake made during a performance typically has fewer consequences than a slip at an audition.

Mock auditions

Staging mock auditions (a.k.a. placebo auditions or dress rehearsals) often helps in getting used to the extra tension. They can take place at home, while performing for family and friends. Some teachers organize mock auditions too. *Tip:* Turn mock auditions into a complete performance, including a formal entrance into the room, presenting yourself, and so on. Also, ask your audience to evaluate your performance afterwards to ensure that they were attentive to every note you played. Scary? That's the idea.

Recording in advance

Recording the pieces you'll be singing at the audition can by very effective.

- Firstly, a recording allows you to listen and evaluate your performance, as it's very difficult to do that while you're singing. And the recorded results can give you the objectivity you need to really assess what you're doing.
- Secondly, a simple recording device can have the same effect as an attentive audience in that it can make you nervous enough

to perhaps make the kind of mistakes you would in front of a real audience. Getting used to the presence of a recording device is quite similar to getting used to an audience, so that makes it effective training.

Evaluate the results

Don't forget to evaluate the recording, and don't listen for mistakes only. Pay close attention to timing, intonation, dynamics, and all other elements that make for a great performance, including tone. Evaluating the latter requires good recording and playback equipment. Tip: First warm up, and then try to sing your prepared pieces and scales right during the first take — just like in real life!

Presentation

Are you required or do you want to dress a certain way for the performance? Then decide beforehand what you're going to wear, how to wear your hair, etc. Don't wait until the day of the show to do this, but get your look together at least the day before.

Sleep

And don't forget: A good night's sleep, or a nap before an afternoon performance, often works wonders!

SHOW TIME

There are many remedies for reducing nerves on the day of your performance too. First of all, leave home early so there's no need to rush, and make sure there's plenty of time to prepare for the performance once you're on site.

Relax

For some, simply repeating the words, 'I'm calm, I'm cool,' is enough to help them relax, but most people need more than this. There are many different techniques, ranging from deep-breathing exercises to meditation, yoga, or special methods like the Alexander Technique. You may also benefit from simple stretching, jumping, and other physical movement, and for some, screaming helps.

Transfer your stress

Another idea is to find a physical release for your stress. For example, take a paperclip along and hold it when you feel nervous, imagining that all of your extra energy is being drawn through your hand into the paperclip — then throw it away before you go onstage.

Warming-up

Warm-up routines (long notes, scales, and so on) not only get you musically prepared to perform, they can also help you relax. Long, slow notes are more effective than up-tempo phrases, obviously. If you feel the need to go through your scales and prepared pieces once more, you probably aren't really ready. Tip: Find a quiet place to prepare, if possible.

Imagine

Many musicians fight their nerves by conjuring calming imagery. They imagine singing at home or on their favorite stage rather than in front of a jury; or they concentrate on a recent holiday, or pretend they're on a deserted island. Others promise themselves that this is their very last performance ever, so they need to give it all — now or never.

Pep talk

Giving yourself a pep talk may help too. But rather than just telling yourself to be cool and calm, tell yourself that you wouldn't even be here if your teacher hadn't thought you were ready — you've earned your way there!

Focus

Don't focus on the outcome of the audition or exam. Instead, concentrate on your music, as that's really what it's all about. What may also help is to make your objective the demonstration of the beauty of the songs you're going to sing, rather than how impressive a vocalist you are. Final tip before going in: Smile when you enter the room. This makes you both look and feel better.

A different type of audience

Auditioners and examiners are a particular kind of audience. They're there to judge your performance, rather than just enjoy the music. Still, it's good to realize that they're there for you: They want you to sing the best you can and they want to make you feel at ease.

Focus

It may help to calm you if you look at your examiners and auditioners the same way you'd look at a 'regular' audience: Tell yourself that they're all very kind people (which they usually are, so this shouldn't be too hard.). Make eye contact with your jurors just as you would any other audience, and smile. And just as you might focus on the people you know, or the ones responding favorably to you in a regular performance, focus on the juror who smiles back at you.

Imagine

Another approach is to completely ignore the audience (imagine that you're singing at home. all by yourself); but realize that this might not work at an audition or an exam. A popular method is to image the audience (large or small, jurors or not) sitting in their underwear, feeling even more uncomfortable than you are onstage. Or think of the audience as non-musicians who will be impressed by every single note you sing or play, or as the ultimate experts who showed up just to hear you…

The first note

Take a couple of seconds before you start. Breathe. Get the tempo of the piece going in your head, or even sing the first few bars in your mind; imagine yourself singing the song. Then it's time for the first note. Make it sound great, and enjoy your performance!

AND MORE

If none of the above works for you, try consulting one of the many books on the subject. Another option is to take a yoga or meditation course, for example, or consider a drama class.

Food and drinks

Various types of food and drink are said to make anxiety worse (e.g., coffee, tea, and other products with caffeine, sugar, or salt), while others help to soothe your nerves. Bananas contain potassium, which helps you relax, and there are various types of calming herbal teas, for example. Alcohol may make you feel more relaxed, but it definitely inhibits motor skills, judgment, and clarity — so avoid drinking alcoholic beverages.

Drugs

Many professional performers take beta blockers (heart medication, actually) to combat their performance anxiety. This type of drug is considered relatively safe, and it works a lot faster than a yoga course and most other relaxation techniques. But you should wonder if music is your thing if you need drugs to do it, even if it's only for high-stress situations, like an audition. Try instead to reduce, if not eliminate, stressors; only do things that make you feel good, and avoid those that induce anxiety. Music is supposed to be fun!

This chapter was taken from Tipbook Music for Kids & Teens *(see page 00*) and adapted for* Tipbook Vocals – The Singing Voice.

13

Reading Music

As an extra, this Tipbook offers you a separate chapter on reading music. Not because you can't sing without it, but because it can help make you a better singer. The information on the next pages is a very condensed rendition of some of the first chapters of Tipbook Music on Paper – Basic Theory (see pages 202 and 223).

There are thousands of singers — even professionals — who don't read music. So why should you?

- You can learn to sing a song **without having heard it** before: your sheet music will tell you what it sounds like.
- You can **sing along** with a band or a choir right away.
- You can also **write music** – melodies for yourself, or charts for the other musicians in your band, for example. Writing something down is easier than remembering it, especially in the long run.
- Talking to other musicians becomes **a lot easier**. You won't be dumbstruck by talk of a B♭-major scale, a fifth, a triplet, or the Mixolydian mode.
- It helps you **understand how music is structured**, and how and why it works the way it does.

By heart

Being able to read music doesn't mean you can't sing without sheet music anymore. The ability to read music simply allows you to sing songs that others have written, but once you know a piece, it may very well sound better if you put the written music away.

HIGH AND LOW

Music is written on a set of five horizontal lines, called the *staff* or *stave*.

- The higher a note is written on the staff, the higher it sounds.
- Lower-sounding notes sit lower on the staff.

It is as simple as that.

One to five

You count the lines of a staff from the bottom up, so the top line is the fifth line.

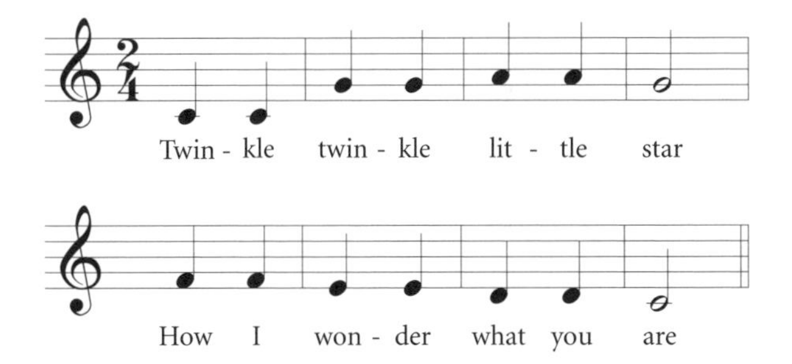

Higher is higher

If you sing 'Twinkle, Twinkle' and look at the notes in the example above, you can clearly see that higher pitched notes sit higher on the staff.

The keyboard

Now take a look at the same song shown on a keyboard. The higher sounding notes are played on keys to the right of the key you started on (the C key).

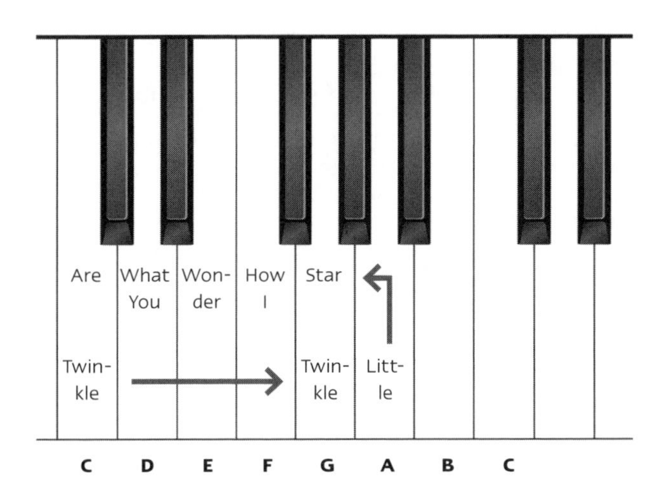

'Twinkle, Twinkle, Little Star': Each syllable is a note.

Letter names

The names of the keys (C, D, E, etcetera) are also shown in the music of 'Twinkle, Twinkle.' As you can see, these letters refer to the keyboard's white keys.

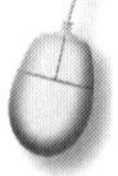

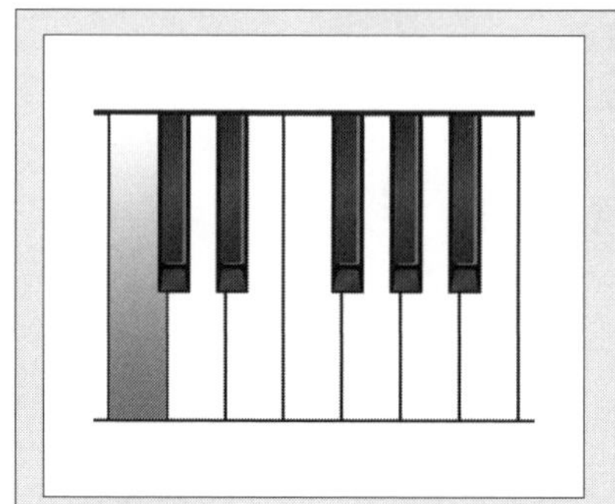

Tipcode MOP-001
Tipcode MOP-001 shows 'Twinkle, Twinkle' played on a piano keyboard.

White notes

This explains why they're often referred to as the *white notes*. The white notes are also known as *natural notes* or *naturals*.

Naturals

The white notes or naturals are C, D, E, F, G, A, B. After this B, the sequence C, D, E etc. starts again.

Do, re, mi

If you sing the ascending scale *do*, *re*, *mi*, *fa*, *so*, *la*, *ti*, *do*, the second *do* is an *octave* higher than the first *do*. Likewise, if you sing the *scale* C, D, E, F, G, A, B, C (which sounds exactly the same as do, re, mi...), the second C is an octave higher than the first.

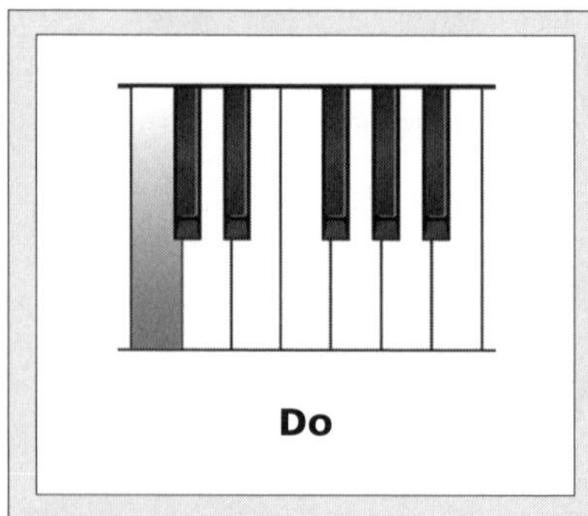

Tipcode MOP-002
This Tipcode plays do, re, mi, fa, so, la, ti, do (or C, D, E, F, G, A, B, C) on a piano keyboard, and then demonstrates that the first and the second do are an octave apart.

On paper

This is what this scale looks like on paper.

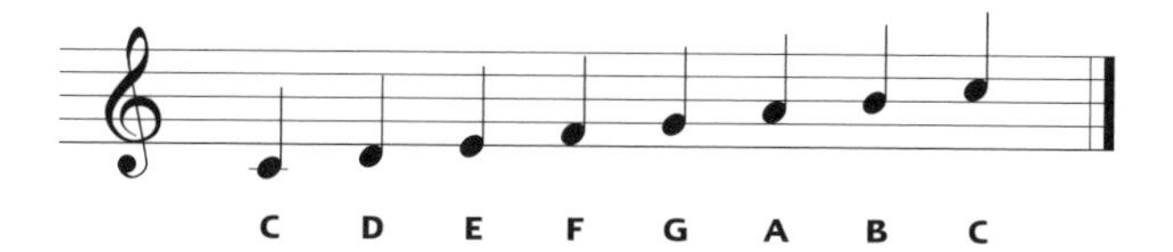

More than one

As you can see, this staff is barely enough to house the eight naturals of one octave — but singers typically have a range of more than two octaves, and you can span no less four octaves from the lowest note of a bass to the highest note of a soprano.

Ledger lines

There are several ways to house all these notes. One is to use *ledger lines.* These small extra lines are used to print notes that are too high or two low for the staff.

Middle C

The lowest note in the example above (the C) is printed on a ledger line. This C sounds when you play the C key in the middle of a piano keyboard. It's known as *Middle C.*

Clefs

Another way to house more notes is to use staffs with different *clefs.* A clef (or *key*) is a symbol at the beginning of a staff. It indicates the position of a given note.
The positions of the other notes can simply be retrieved from this starting point.

Two main clefs

The two most commonly used clefs are the G-clef and the F-clef. Singers typically use only one of these clefs.

G-clef

The curly clef that you saw in the musical examples before, is called the *G-clef.* The curl in the center of this clef indicates the position of the note G above Middle C.
In this clef, Middle C is written on a the first ledger line below the staff.

Treble clef or G-clef

Treble clef

The staff with the G-clef is used for the higher sounding notes — the notes on the right hand side of a piano keyboard, for example. Most vocal music is written in this clef too, and so is music for higher sounding instruments such as trumpets and violins. That's why the G-clef is also known as the *treble clef*.

F-clef

The two dots of the *F-clef* indicate the note F below Middle C. Middle C is on the first ledger line above this staff.

Bass clef or F-clef

Bass clef

The staff with the F-clef is used for lower pitches (*e.g.*, bass and baritone voices, double bass, tuba...). Therefore it's also known as the *bass clef*.

Again: Middle C

Piano music always uses two staffs: one with the G-clef, and a second staff with the F-clef below it. Middle C is on the ledger line in the *middle* of these two clefs.

Pianists read two staffs simultaneously.

Notes and keys

The diagram below shows the middle section of a piano keyboard and the corresponding notes on the staffs.

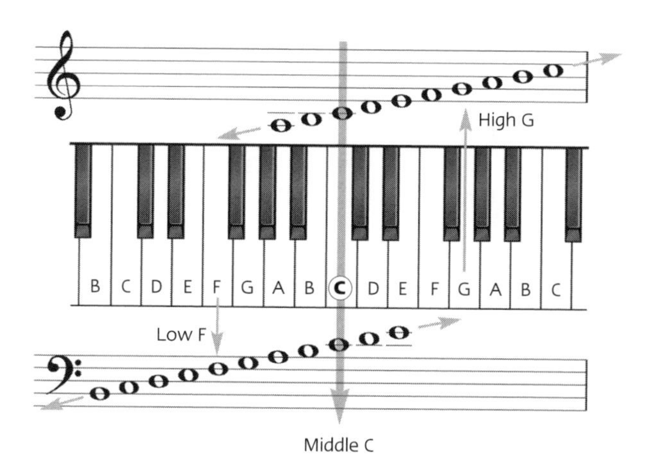

Natural notes in the bass (F) and treble (G) clefs.

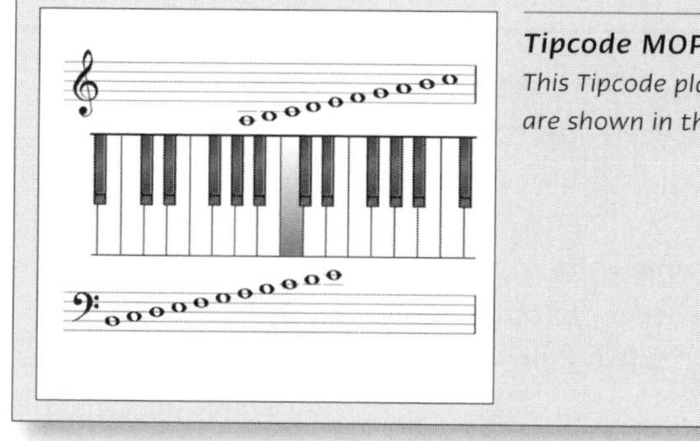

Tipcode MOP-006

This Tipcode plays the notes that are shown in the illustration above.

Different

As you may have noticed, the notes sit on different places on each staff. For example, the middle line of the treble staff indicates a B. The middle line of the bass clef indicates a D. As said before, singers typically use one clef only — so all you have to learn is to read the notes in that one staff.

An octave higher

Notes that require more than three ledger lines are hard to read, and using more than two clefs would be confusing. That's why there's another solution to write down higher or lower sounding parts: It's a symbol that tells you to play or sing a section one or even two octaves higher or lower than written. The symbol 8va tells you to sing or play an octave higher than written; 8vb tells you to sing or play an octave lower.

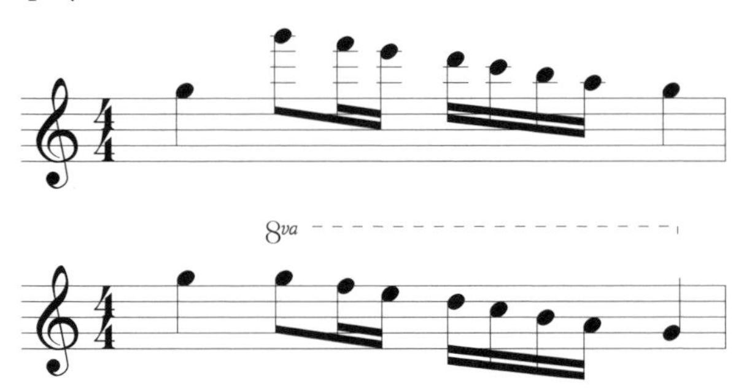

Two ways of writing the same melody. The one below is much easier to read.

LONG AND SHORT

The position of a note on the staff shows you which note to sing. The look of the note itself tells you how long it's supposed to last.

Tap your foot

If you're singing a song, you can always tap your foot in time to what you hear. Once every few taps you may hear or feel some sort of accent. Just sing the two following songs:

1 - 2 **1** - 2 **1** - 2 **1**
Yan - kee Doo - dle went to town.

1 - 2 - 3 **1** - 2 - 3 **1** - 2-(3)
(My) Bon - nie lies o - ver the o - cean.

Oompa

The 'accents' in 'Yankee Doodle' subdivide the song into groups of two taps or beats. 'My Bonnie' is divided into groups of three beats. These subdivisions determine the rhythmic 'feel' of the music. Dance to it and you'll feel it: *Oompa oompa* makes you move differently than *oompapa oompapa* does.

Bars

Most music is divided into such groups of two, three, or four beats. Each group of beats is called a *bar* or a *measure*.

Clap along

If you clap along as you sing the first four words of 'Baa Baa Black Sheep' you will probably clap on each word. 'Baa Baa Black Sheep' is four beats.

Quarter note

The example below shows how these four beats look on paper. Each beat in that first bar is represented by a black bullet with a stem, known as a *quarter note*. In most songs, the quarter note represents one beat.

Four in a bar

In most songs, there are four quarter notes to every bar. This is shown at the beginning of the staff as $\frac{4}{4}$.

Longer and shorter

The second bar of 'Baa Baa Black Sheep' has four words that last shorter than one beat. The last word ('wool') lasts longer than

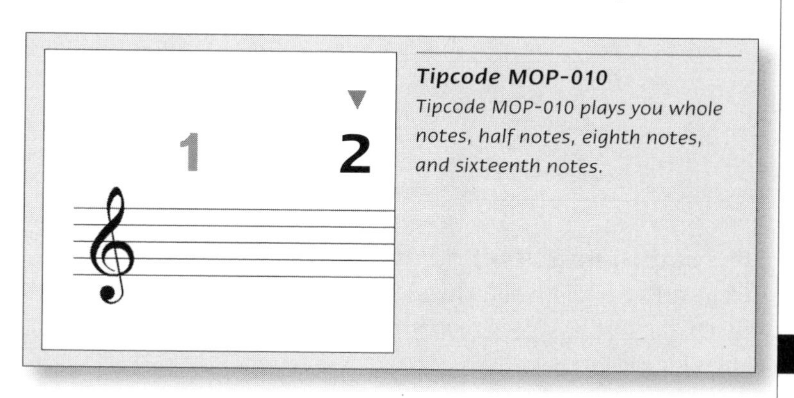

Tipcode MOP-010

Tipcode MOP-010 plays you whole notes, half notes, eighth notes, and sixteenth notes.

one beat. To indicate these longer and shorter durations, there are whole notes, half notes, eighth notes, sixteenth notes, and other notes.

The whole note: four beats in 4/4

In 4/4, the *whole note* lasts four beats. If you sing such a note, you keep on singing for four beats.

A whole note lasts four beats in 4/4.

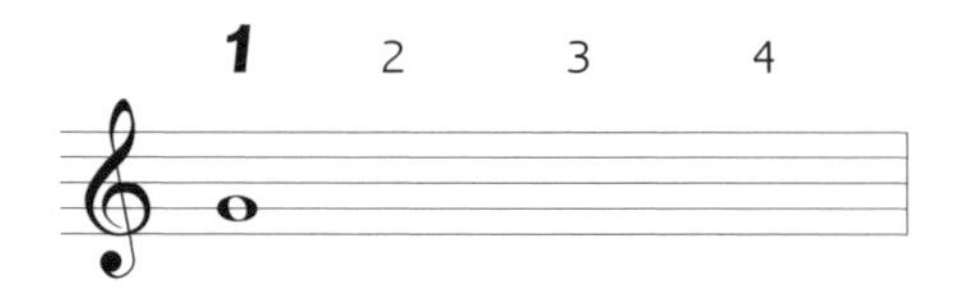

The half note: two beats in 4/4

The *half note* lasts half as long as a whole note: two beats. Two half notes fill up a four-beat bar.

The half note: two beats in 4/4.

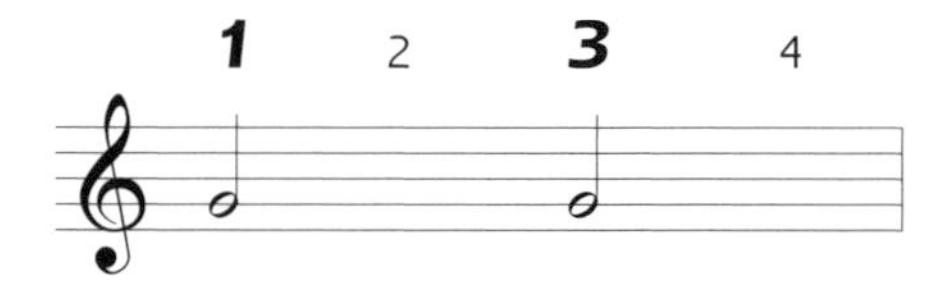

The quarter note: one beat in 4/4

In 4/4, the *quarter note* lasts one beat. If you tap along with your foot, sing one note to each tap.

The quarter note: one beatin 4/4.

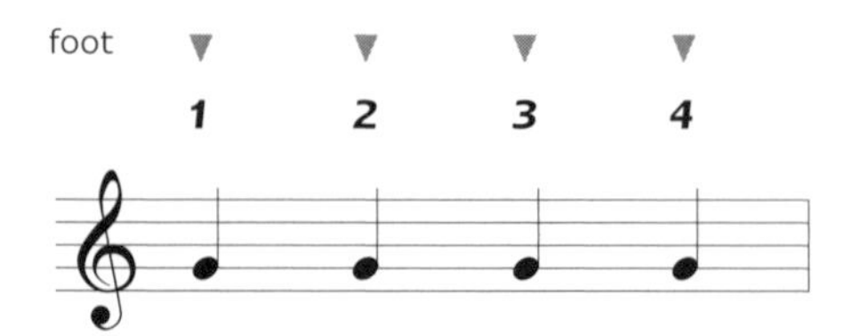

The eighth note: half a beat in 4/4

There are two *eighth notes* in one quarter note. In 'Bah Bah Black Sheep' the words 'have you any' are eighth notes: There are two notes for each beat.

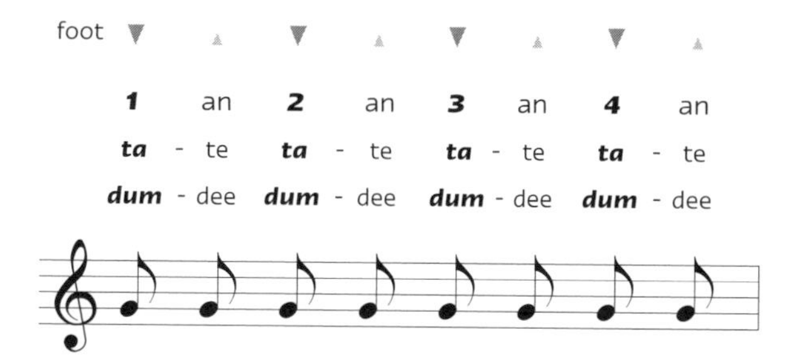

An eighth note lasts half a beat in 4/4.

Sixteenth note: a quarter beat in 4/4

There are four *sixteenth notes* to one beat. Sixteenth notes sound twice as fast as eighth notes.

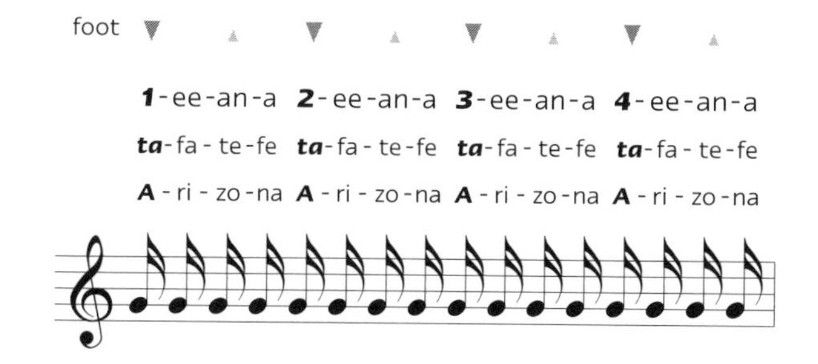

A sixteenth note lasts a quarter of a beat in 4/4.

Heads, stems, and flags

How long a note lasts is referred to as its *note value*. The note's looks show you its note value.

the note	its name	its parts	lasts (in 4/4)
𝅝	whole note *(semibreve)*	open head	four beats
𝅗𝅥	half note *(minim)*	open head and stem	two beats
♩	quarter note *(crotchet)*	closed head and stem	one beat
♪	eighth note *(quaver)*	closed head, stem, and flag	half a beat
𝅘𝅥𝅯	sixteenth note *(semiquaver)*	closed head, stem, and two flags	quarter beat

Every note is built up out of one, two, or three parts: an open or a closed head, a stem, and a flag, as you can see in the table on the previous page. This table also lists the British names for the different note values (in parentheses).

BAR LINES AND TIME SIGNATURES

The bars or measures in a piece of music are divided by vertical lines: the *bar lines.*

Time signature

The number of beats per bar is always indicated at the beginning. 'Bah Bah Black Sheep' begins with $\frac{4}{4}$, pronounced as *four-four.* This is the *time signature.* It tells you how many beats there are in each bar, and which note equals one beat.

Common time

This particular time signature, $\frac{4}{4}$, is very common in Western music. It's so common, in fact, that it's also known as *common time.*

Four-four bar

In a piece in $\frac{4}{4}$, each bar lasts as long as four quarter notes. So it may contain four quarter notes, but also one whole note, or two quarter notes and a half note, and so on, as long as it all adds up to $\frac{4}{4}$. An example? A half note + a quarter note + two eighth notes fill up one $\frac{4}{4}$ bar. It's just a matter of basic math: $1/2 + 1/4 + 2/8 = 4/4$.

The upper number

The upper number in the time signature tells you how many beats there are in each bar. In a piece in $\frac{4}{4}$ there are four beats per bar.

Lower number and counting unit

The lower number indicates which note lasts one beat. In $\frac{4}{4}$, that's a quarter note: $1/4 + 1/4 + 1/4 + 1/4 = 4/4$. This implies that you count the piece in quarter notes: The quarter note is *the counting unit.*

Three-four

'My Bonnie Lies Over the Ocean' doesn't have four, but three quarter notes to every bar. Its time signature is $\frac{3}{4}$, or *three-four,* sometimes known as *waltz time.*

'My Bonnie': three beats per bar.

Two or five

There are more time signatures than just $\frac{4}{4}$ and $\frac{3}{4}$. For example, time signatures with two beats per bar, such as $\frac{2}{4}$; (*e.g.*, 'Twinkle, Twinkle') or five beats per bar, such as $\frac{5}{4}$.

Another counting unit

Likewise, there are time signatures based on another counting unit; usually the eighth note. In $\frac{3}{8}$ there are three eighth notes in every bar. There's more about time signatures in *Tipbook Music on Paper.*

$\frac{4}{4}$ 1 2 3 4

$\frac{4}{4}$ 1 2 3 4

$\frac{4}{4}$ 1 2 3 4

$\frac{4}{4}$ 1 2 3 4

$\frac{4}{4}$ 1 2 3 4

One whole note, two half notes, four quarter notes, eight eighth notes, sixteen sixteenth notes: They all last four beats in $\frac{4}{4}$, filling up one bar.

C and ₵

Instead of $\frac{4}{4}$, the symbol C is used quite often: It's the C of *common time*. The symbol ₵ indicates a $\frac{2}{2}$ time signature, which is also known as *cut common time* or *alla breve*. In $\frac{2}{2}$, the half note is the counting unit. In other words, a half note equals one beat.

Beams

Sequences of eighth, sixteenth, and shorter notes can be made easier to read if their individual flags are replaced by beams.

Beam = flag

A beam has the same value as a flag. An eighth note has one flag, so eighth notes are joined by a single beam. Sixteenth notes have two flags, so they're joined with a double beam.

RESTS

Each of the preceding examples assigns one or more notes to every beat. However, there's more to music than notes. The rests are just as important – silence, next to sound. A rest means you actually stop singing for a moment. Just like notes, there are whole, half, quarter, and shorter rests.

the rest	its name	lasts as long as	lasts (in $\frac{4}{4}$)
	whole rest *(semibreve rest)*	whole note	four beats
	half rest *(minim rest)*	half note	two beats
	quarter rest *(crotchet rest)*	quarter note	one beat
	eighth rest *(quaver rest)*	eighth note	half a beat
	sixteenth rest *(semiquaver rest)*	sixteenth note	quarter beat

Rectangles and tags

In $\frac{4}{4}$, a whole rest lasts four beats, just like a whole note. Likewise, a half rests lasts two beats, etc.

DOTS AND TIES

Notes can be made longer by adding a dot. A note followed by a dot is 1.5 times its original length. These dots are known as *augmentation dots.*

Two + one = three

In $\frac{4}{4}$ a half note with a dot lasts 1.5 x two beats = three beats. A dotted quarter note lasts a beat and-a-half. And so on.

Ties

A tie extends a note by joining it to another note of the same pitch. If two notes are joined by a tie, the second note is simply held on, instead of being sung separately.

Tipcode MOP-012

Here is a short melody that uses ties.

TRIPLETS AND OTHER -PLETS

As you have seen, each note can be divided into two, four or more shorter notes (quarter notes, eighth notes, sixteenth notes…). But you can also divide notes into three or five, for example.

Triplets

If you divide a quarter note into two, you get two eighth notes. When you divide it into three, you get an eighth-note triplet. Triplets are marked with the number 3 above or below the three notes, sometimes with a square bracket or a curved line.

Sextuplets

Notes can also be divided into six (*sextuplet*), for example.

SHARPS AND FLATS

The natural or white notes discussed above are just seven of the twelve notes in an octave. The other five – the black notes – are named in relation to these white notes.

TIPCODE

Tipcode MOP-017

Twinkle Twinkle starting on F. The B sounds too high.

TIPCODE

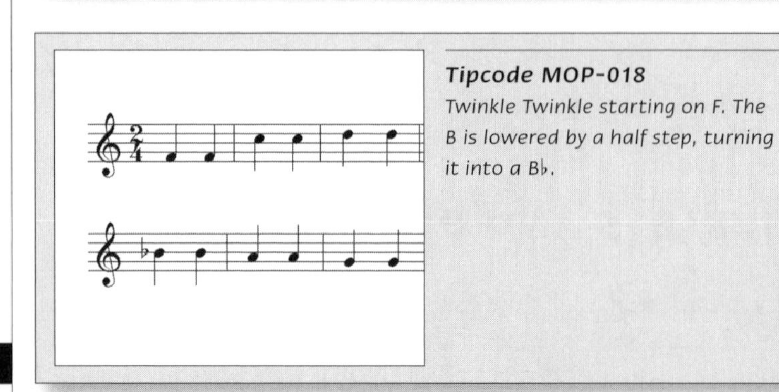

Tipcode MOP-018

Twinkle Twinkle starting on F. The B is lowered by a half step, turning it into a B♭.

Twinkle, Twinkle

On page 181, *Twinkle, Twinkle* was played starting on C. If you play the same song but you would start on the F key, something strange will happen: The B, on the words 'how I,' sounds too high.

Lower the B

The solution is to lower the B by a half step. On a keyboard you play this lowered B by hitting the black key just to the left of it.

Flats

The lowered B is indicated with a flat (♭). To play a flatted note on a keyboard instrument, you simply move one black or white key to the left. That note sounds a half step lower. Here is 'Twinkle, Twinkle,' starting on F, now with a B♭ (pronounced as *B-flat*) to make it sound right. The other natural notes can be lowered in exactly the same way.

Twinkle, Twinkle – once more

If you would begin 'Twinkle, Twinkle' on a D and use white keys only, you'd hear that the F on the word 'wonder' sounds too low.

Too low

The solution is to raise the F a half step. On a keyboard you do so by playing the black note to the right of the F. This is the note F♯, pronounced F-sharp.

Every note

Of course, every note in the octave can be lowered with a flat or raised with a sharp.

ACCIDENTALS AND KEY SIGNATURES

Sharps and flats are *chromatic signs*. You may find chromatic signs in one or more bars of a piece, as well as at the very beginning, next to the clef.

One bar

A sharp or a flat in a bar raises or flattens the following notes in that bar. In 'Twinkle, Twinkle' on D (previous page), a single sharp raises both F's in the sixth bar.

Accidentals

When used this way, sharps and flats are called accidentals. An accidental applies to the notes at the same line or space within that same bar only.

The whole piece

You'll often see one or more sharps or flats at the very beginning of a piece, next to the clef. These sharps or flats apply to the whole song and to every octave. If there's one flat next to the clef, every B in the piece should be lowered to B♭, not just the ones at the same line or space as the symbol.

Key signature

The sharps or flats at the clef don't just tell you which notes to lower or to raise: They also indicate the *key signature* of the piece, or what key a piece is in. There's more information on keys and key signatures in *Tipbook Music on Paper* (see page 202)

Which notes

A key signature can contain one, two, three, or more sharps or flats – or none, if the piece is in the key of C. Each sharp or flat clearly indicates the note it refers to: It is on the same line or space as that note.

Tipcode MOP-019

The two sharps in the key signature tell you that all C's and all F's should be raised.

Natural signs

Flats and sharps can be suspended within a single bar by the natural sign (♮).

LOUD AND SOFT

A chart not only tells you which notes to sing and how long they should last. It also tells you how softly or loudly you should sing them.

Dynamics

Variations in volume are called dynamics. On paper, dynamic markings indicate how loudly or softly you should sing. Dynamics are usually indicated by Italian words or their abbreviations. These are the standard *dynamic markings*:

ppp	pianisissimo	very, very soft
pp	pianissimo	very soft
p	piano	soft
p	mezzo piano	moderately soft
mf	mezzo forte	moderately loud
f	forte	loud; strong
ff	fortissimo	very loud; very strong
fff	fortisissimo	very, very loud; very, very strong

Until the next

Dynamic markings are always under the first note they apply to. From that note onward you keep singing at the indicated volume until you come across the next dynamic marking.

Gradually

There are also dynamic markings that tell you to get gradually louder (*crescendo*: ——) or softer (*decrescendo*: ——).

More bars

A (de)crescendo that's stretched over a larger number of bars is often indicated by the word '(de)crescendo,' or the abbreviation *cresc.*, followed by a dotted line. The (de)crescendo ends where that line stops.

English

In non-classical music, dynamics are often indicated in English. These terms, which have not been standardized, are often more descriptive than simply 'loud' or 'soft'.

TEMPO

There are two main ways of indicating the tempo of a piece of music – with numbers or Italian terms.

Beats per minute

For many songs, the tempo is indicated in *beats per minute* (*BPM*). If the chart shows (♩ = 120), this tells you that there should be 120 quarter notes in a minute (*i.e.*, 120 BPM, which equals two beats per second!).

Italian

The other way to indicate tempo is to use a selection of Italian terms. Most metronomes show the common Italian tempo

Italian	Translation	Metronome Marking
Largo	very slow	♩ = 40-60
Adagio	slow	♩ = 66-76
Andante	walking, relaxed tempo	♩ = 76-108
Moderato	medium tempo	♩ = 108-120
Allegro	fast	♩ = 120-168
Presto	very fast	♩ = 168-200

markings and how they relate to BPM. The previous page shows some of these markings.

English

Of course, English words or phrases can be used to indicate the tempo as well, ranging from the basic 'fast' to more musical expressions such as *ballad* or *up tempo.*

ARTICULATION

You can 'pronounce' or articulate notes in different ways, just like words. A set of *articulation signs* or *articulation symbols* shows you how to articulate the notes you're reading. Some examples:

Accents

The best known articulation sign is the accent. This horizontal 'V' above or below a note, tells you to emphasize it by singing it a little louder.

Staccato

A dot above or below a note indicated that you should sing it staccato: very short and clipped.

Legato

Legato (literally 'bound') is the opposite of staccato: The notes are

Tipcode MOP-027

Here's the difference between four regular quarter notes and the same notes with a legato slur.

held on slightly longer than usual so there is very little or no space between them. A legato is marked with a slur: a curved line that binds notes together into groups.

SECTION MARKINGS AND REPEAT SIGNS

Songs usually consist of a number of different sections, *e.g.*, verses and choruses. Often, these sections repeat a number of times, or the song might skip backwards or forwards to a particular point. There are various special markings and repeat signs that act like signposts, directing you around a piece of music.

Intro, outro, bridge

Songs or other pieces of music usually have more sections than a verses and choruses. An *intro* is the first section of a song, before it really gets going — which is usually when the vocals come in. The term *outro* is often used for the final section, usually when the singing has stopped. A *bridge* literally bridges two different sections.

Section markings

The various sections of a piece are often indicated by letters. These section markings are also known as rehearsal marks, as that's when they're often used: Instead of playing or singing a piece from the top after every mistake, the band leader or conductor may suggest to 'take it from H,' for example. Section markings or rehearsal marks are usually written in small boxes above the staff.

Bar numbers

A number placed above a bar line – on its own, in a circle or in a box – usually indicates the number of the following bar, counting from the beginning of the piece.

Section lines

Sections are often marked by section lines (thin, double bar lines).

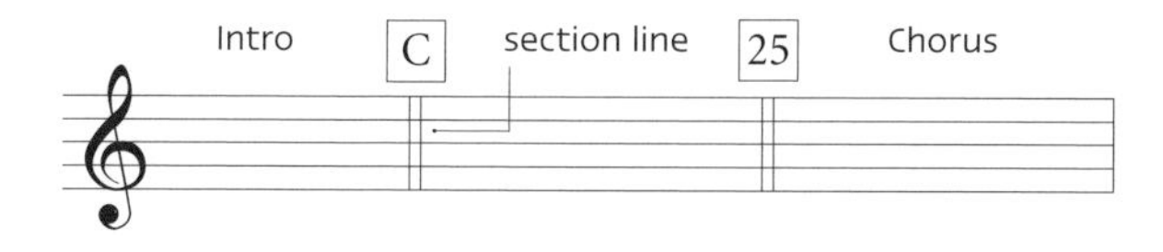

Names, letters, or numbers are used to identify the various parts of a piece.

Double bar line

The double bar line (a normal bar line followed by a thick one) indicates the end of a piece. It is also used in repeat signs, which are explained in the next section.

Repeat signs

Repeat signs tell you to repeat one or more bars, or a section of the piece.

Repeating

A section that should be played or sung twice is usually marked with two repeat signs, one on either end of the section. The illustration below shows what they look like. There are also symbols that tell you to repeat the previous bar or the previous two bars.

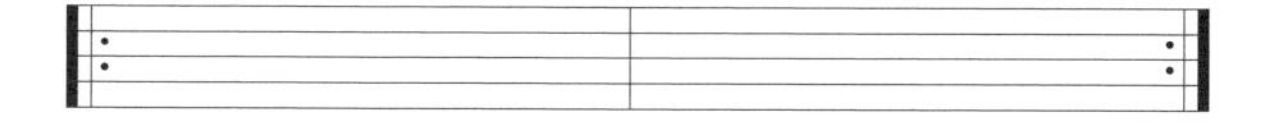

Repeat from the beginning.

First and second ending

Sometimes a repeated section ends differently the second time around. This is indicated with square brackets marked 1 and 2, as in the example below. You end the section the first time around by singing the bar or bars marked 1 (the *first ending* or *prima volta*). When you get to this point the second time, you skip to the bar or bars marked 2 (*second ending* or *seconda volta*).

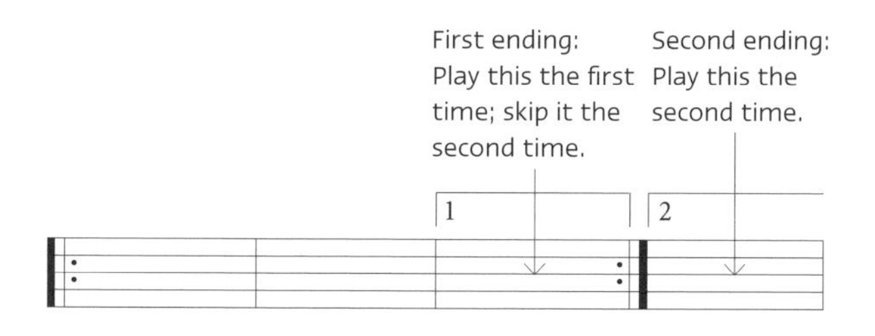

First and second ending.

Skipping around

A variety of symbols, words and abbreviations is used to indicate that you have to skip from one part of a piece to another.

Da Capo

Da Capo (D.C.) means that you go back to the beginning of a piece and repeat everything you sung so far. The intro shouldn't be included unless it is indicated that you should. When you reach D.C. the second time, ignore it and continue with the music that follows.

Dal Segno

Dal Segno (D.S.) means 'from the sign.' When you reach a D.S., you go back to the 𝄋 sign (the *segno*), which always precedes the D.S. You repeat the bars between the segno and the D.S. once, and ignore D.S. the second time you reach it.

Al Coda

Da Capo Al Coda means you have to go back to the beginning of the piece (D.C.), and then sing on until you reach the coda sign 𝄌 CODA. This sign tells you to skip to the coda, which is a section at the end of the piece, marked with that word.

Fine

Al Fine means 'to the end.' Da Capo al Fine (or D.C. al Fine) means go back to the beginning, and then finish the piece where you see the word Fine. This Fine is not the last bar of the printed music, but it is the end of the piece. You should pronounce the Italian Fine somewhat like 'Feenuh'.

TIPBOOK MUSIC ON PAPER

This chapter was taken from T*ipbook Music on Paper – Basic Theory*, a publication that tells you a lot more about reading music, and the system behind all those notes: about intervals and key signatures, about major, minor, and other types of scales, about time signatures, and much more. The book also tells you how easy it is to transpose a song (rewriting it a few notes higher or lower, so you can sing those lowest or highest notes that would otherwise be out of your range), it helps you to determine the key of a song, and provides you with an accessible glossary of terms and more than fifty unique Tipcodes that allow you to hear what you read. For more information, please see page 223.

Glossary

This glossary contains short definitions of most of the vocal terms used in this book. The numbers refer to the pages where the term is covered in more detail. There are also some words you won't find on the previous pages, but which you may well come across elsewhere.

A cappella
Unaccompanied singing; just vocals, no other instruments.

Adduction
Bringing your vocal folds together, closing the glottis. Antonym: *Abduction.*

Altus
Male alto. See: *Voice types.*

Articulation
Changing the shape of your resonator to create vowels, consonants, and other sounds is known as articulation.

Articulators, articulatory system
Your lower jaw, lips, tongue, soft palate (velum), used to articulate or form vowels, consonants and other sounds. You also use your articulators to influence the timbre of your voice.

Arytenoids
Your vocal folds are attached to two small, rocking and gliding cartilages at the back of your throat: the arytenoids.

Attack
The way you 'attack' or initiate a vowel. Also referred to as *onset.* See also: *Glottal attack.*

Back-electret
(Almost) all modern condenser microphone are *back-electret* condenser microphones. For singers, this technical detail is not really relevant.

Bass, baritone
See: *Voice types.*

Bell register
See: *Whistle register.*

Belting
Belting can be defined as a safe way to sing loudly.

Break
See: *Passaggio.*

Breath support
Supporting your breath, mainly by keeping your diaphragm low while singing. Essential for good singing (loud, soft, in tune, good timbre, stamina, and so on) in all styles of music.

Breathing
To sing well, you need to breathe well — and that's not necessarily what feels natural to you.

Cardioid
See: *Pickup pattern.*

Castrato
Singer who has been unmanned to preserve his boyhood voice. Castratos used to sing in the church (thirteenth–nineteenth century) and in the opera (mainly seventeenth and eighteenth century).

Chest register
One of the many names for the heavy, low, or modal register of the human voice. People usually speak in their chest register. Men and

female non-classical singers usually sing in their chest register as well.

Chest resonance
Vibrations in the chest as a result of the overtone and/or fundamental frequencies of your voice.

Chest voice
Often used to indicate either chest resonance or chest register.

Condenser microphone
More precise, clear, direct, crisp, and sensitive than a *dynamic microphone*. Used in studios, and increasingly onstage.

Counter tenor
See: *Voice types.*

Covering
Lowering the voice box to make vowels sound warmer, darker, or rounder. Covering is also referred to as *vowel mutation* or *modification.*

Cricoid
Ring-shaped cartilage that sits on your windpipe. One of the two largest parts of the larynx.

Diaphragm
1. Dome-shaped muscle, bottom up, that separates your lungs from your abdomen.
2. Extremely thin, flexible plate in a microphone. Sound makes the diaphragm move.
   These movements translate into electric signals, which can be amplified.

Dramatical
A dramatical tenor has a heavier or darker timbre than a *lyrical tenor.* See: *Lyrical.*

Dynamic microphone
Most popular microphone for onstage use. Rugged, reliable, affordable. Typically produces a warmer, rounder, mellower sound than a *condenser microphone.*

Epiglottis
Flexible cartilage that covers and protects the vocal folds when you swallow.

Falsetto register
Highest and lightest of the two main registers of the singing voice. Sometimes used for male voices only, in which case the female 'falsetto' is usually referred to as *head register* or *head voice.* Both terms are defined in other ways too. Also known as *light register.*

Feedback
The loud *skreee* you may hear when a microphone picks up sound from your monitors or other speakers.

Frequency response
The way a microphone responds to various frequency ranges, *i.e.*, low, high and middle frequencies.

Full head
Term used to indicate the high range of the modal or chest register.

Fundamental pitch
If you sing an A4, your glottis opens

and closes 440 time per second (440Hz). This is the fundamental pitch, or fundamental frequency, of that note. Like any other instrument, your voice generates a series of weaker sounding overtones, each at a multitude of the fundamental frequency. At 440Hz this would be 880Hz, 1,320Hz, and so on.

Glottal attack, glottal initiation
Initiating a vowel with a closed glottis.

Glottis
The opening between the vocal folds. You close your glottis by bringing the vocal folds together, just like you close your mouth by bringing your lips together.

Grunt register
See: *Vocal fry.*

Head register
One of the terms indicating the higher or lighter of the two main registers of the singing voice. Also known as *falsetto* or *light register.*

Head resonance
Vibrations in the head as a result of the overtone or fundamental frequencies of your voice.

Head voice
May indicate both *head register* and *head resonance.*

High C
For tenors, High C is C5; for sopranos it's C6, one octave higher. When singing C6, the glottis opens and closes no less than 1,056 times per second.

Hypercardioid
See: *Pickup pattern.*

International Phonetic Alphabet (IPA)
Special alphabet that indicates the sound of vowels and consonants of languages from all over the world.

IPA
See: *International Phonetic Alphabet.*

Larynx
Complex structure in the throat, housing the vocal folds. Also known as *voice box.*

Legit, legitimate voice
A classical or head type of sound in Broadway singing.

Light register
See: *Falsetto and Head register.*

Lyrical
A lyrical voice is a flexible and versatile voice with a light timbre; a dramatical tenor has a darker and heavier timbre than a lyrical tenor.

Messa di voce
Popular singer's exercise, varying the loudness at a given pitch and vowel from soft to loud and back.

Mezzo-soprano
See: *Voice types.*

Mixed voice
Defined in many different ways. This 'mix' between chest and head voice is essential in some schools of singing, while others will tell you there's no such thing as a mixed voice.

Modal register
Another name to indicate the heavy or chest register. Both men and women usually speak in this register; most male and non-classical female singers sing in it.

Mutation
The physical development from a boy's to a man's voice, and from a girl's to a woman's voice.

Omnidirectional
An omnidirectional microphone picks up sound from all angles. Usually used in studios.

Onset
See: *Attack.*

Overtone singing
Special vocal technique, restricting the fundamental pitch and accenting the overtones. See: *Overtones.*

Overtones
Each fundamental pitch you sing is accompanied by a range of overtones in different intensities. The difference between the vowels A and O, for example, is 'simply' a matter of different overtone intensities, and so are the different timbres you can create.

Passaggio
Also known as *register transition, register change, gear change, bridge,* or *break*: where the human voice moves from one register to the next, and back.

Phantom power
Condenser microphones need power, which is usually supplied through the mic's cable. This is known as phantom power.

Pickup pattern
A mic's pickup pattern tells you where it is most sensitive and where it's not. Also known as *polar pattern* or *sensitivity field.* Most live microphones have a *cardioid* or *supercardioid* pickup pattern.

Polar pattern
See: *Pickup pattern.*

Polyp
Enlarged area on the vocal folds, typically caused by overusing the voice, acid reflux, or smoking.

Pop filter
Mainly reduces the noise of plosive consonants (P, B, and so on). Many vocal mics have a built-in pop filter.

Pronunciation
The way you make words sound, using your articulators.

Proximity effect
The effect of added bass and warmth (and boominess) that you hear when getting closer to a unidirectional microphone.

Pulse register
See: *Vocal fry.*

Register
Most experts agree that the singing voice has two main registers: heavy, chest, or modal; and light, head or falsetto.
The difference in sound between these registers is a result of your vocal folds vibrating in a different way. There are more registers than these two; some schools of thought say there's only one register, though.

Register transition
See: *Passaggio.*

Release
How you end a tone or a word.

Response pattern
See: *Pickup pattern.*

Sensitivity field
See: *Pickup pattern.*

Soprano
See: *Voice types.*

Supercardioid
See: *Pickup pattern.*

Tenor
See: *Voice types.*

Thyroid
Your vocal folds run from the arytenoids, in the back, to the inside of the thyroid. If the thyroid rocks forward on the *cricoid*, it stretches the vocal folds.

Trachea
Wind pipe.

Transient response
A transient is the very first attack noise of a sound. The faster a microphone responds to transients, the more precise and direct it will pick up the subtlest nuances of your voice.

UHF
One of the two main frequency ranges for wireless microphones.

Unidirectional
A unidirectional microphone doesn't pick up sound from one direction only, as its name suggests, but it's very sensitive in some areas, while rejecting or reducing sound from other angles. This is reflected in the mic's pickup pattern. See: *Pickup pattern.*

VHF
One of the two main frequency ranges for wireless microphones.

Vibrato
Slight pitch fluctuation.

Vocal cords
See: *Vocal folds.*

Vocal folds
Your vocal folds generate the sound of your voice. Simply put, they're muscle tissue covered with mucous membrane. You close and open your *glottis* with your vocal folds.

Vocal fry
The very lowest notes of the human

voice. Also known as *pulse register* or *grunt register*; the terms used clearly indicate the sound in this register.

Vocal microphone, vocalist microphone
Microphone for singers.

Vocal nodes, vocal nodules
Small growths on your vocal folds. Can be cured with rest, if discovered in time. Always appear in pairs, one on each fold.

Vocal tract
Your pharynx, mouth, and nasal cavities; the *resonator* of your vocal instrument. This is where your voice gets its specific sound or timbre. You produce all your vowels, consonants, and numerous other sounds by changing the shape of your vocal tract or resonator, using your articulators. See also: *Articulators.*

Voice box
See: *Larynx.*

Voice range profile
Series of measurements of the notes in your singing range, sung at various volume levels. Also known as *phonetogram*. Used for voice classification.

Voice types
There are various voice types, each with a specific range and timbre. The main male voice types, from low and dark to high and bright, are *bass*, *baritone*, *tenor*, and *counter tenor*, also known as *altus*. The main female voice types, in similar order, are *contralto*, *alto*, *mezzo-soprano*, and *soprano*. The opera distinguishes even more types of voices.

Vowel modification, vowel mutation
See: *Covering.*

Warm-up
Essential exercises to prepare the voice.

Whistle register
The very highest register of the (female) voice. Also known as *bell register* or *flute register.*

Windshield
Microphone accessory. Mainly reduces wind and sibilant noise.

TIPCODE LIST

The Tipcodes in this book offer easy access to short movies, photo series, soundtracks, and other additional information at www.tipbook.com. For your convenience, the Tipcodes in this Tipbook have been listed below.

Tipcode	Topic	Page	Chapter
VOCALS-001	A puff of air	**6**	**2**
VOCALS-002	Vibrating vocal folds and balloon	**7**	**2**
VOCALS-003	Low and high notes	**8**	**2**
VOCALS-004	The break	**15**	**2**
VOCALS-005	Different timbres	**15**	**2**
VOCALS-006	Breathy tone	**41**	**4**
VOCALS-007	Open throat, tight throat	**45**	**4**
VOCALS-008	Overtone singing	**46**	**4**
VOCALS-009	Nasal timbre	**61**	**4**
VOCALS-011	Messa di voce	**68**	**4**
VOCALS-012	Pitch bend and fall-off	**71**	**4**
VOCALS-013	Vibrato	**81**	**4**
VOCALS-014	Non-classical falsetto	**86**	**5**
VOCALS-015	Different timbres	**89**	**5**
VOCALS-016	E4: a 3-millisecond cycle	**90**	**5**
VOCALS-017	Equalizing the passaggio: short scales	**94**	**5**
VOCALS-018	Belting	**95**	**5**
VOCALS-019	Same notes, different timbres	**99**	**6**
VOCALS-020	Warm-up exercises	**119**	**8**
VOCALS-021	Effects	**161**	**10**
VOCALS-022	Pitch correction	**163**	**10**

Magazines

There is a limited number of specialized magazines for vocalists. If you want to read more about singers, or if you are interested in reviews of microphones and other singers' equipment, please consult general music magazines.

- *Classical Singer*, classicalsinger.com; subscriptions@classicalsinger.com
- *Journal of Singing*, National Association of Teachers of Singing (NATS), www.nats.org
- *The Journal of Voice* (research and study of the human voice), www.voicefoundation.org
- *Singer & Musician*, www.ilivetoplay.net
- *Singing News*, www.singingnews.com
- *Sing Out!* (The Folk Song Magazine), www.singout.org
- *The Singer Magazine* (UK; from cabaret to grand opera), www.rhinegold.co.uk
- *Opera Now Magazine* (UK), www.rhinegold.co.uk

Books

There are numerous books on singing. Some focus on classical singing, others on non-classical singing, and a few deal with both. Some books mainly offer background information, others are method books, and a few can be used both ways. The following is just a selection.

- *Bel Canto: Principles and Practices*, Cornelius Reid (The Joseph Patelson Music House, New York, first published 1950, fifth printing 1990; 264 pages; ISBN 0 91528 201 1).
- *Complete Handbook of Voice Training*, Richard Alderson (Prentice Hall Trade, 1979; ISBN 0 1316 307 3).
- *Complete Vocal Technique*, Cathrine Sadolin (Shout Publishing ApS Denmark, 2000; ISBN 87 9867 972 4).
- *Discover Your Voice: How to Develop Healthy Voice Habits*, Oren L. Brown (Singular Publishing Group, 1996; 300 pages; ISBN 1 56593 704 X).

- *Foundations in Singing – A Basic Textbook in Vocal Technique and Song Interpretation*, Van A. Christy and John Glenn Paton (McGraw-Hill, 1997; 191 pages; ISBN 0 697 12566 1).
- *Learning to Sing Non-Classical Music*, Ronald Coombs and Robert Bowker (Prentice Hall, NJ, 1995; 147 pages; ISBN 0 13 010729 8).
- *New Vocal Repertory: An Introduction*, Jane Manning (Clarendon Press, Oxford, 1994; ISBN 0 19 816413 0).
- *Power Performance for Singers: Transcending the Barriers*, Shirlee Emmons and Alma Thomas (Oxford University Press, 1998; ISBN 0 19 511224 5).
- *Principles of Pop Singing*, Jodie Lyons, Lanelle Stevenson (Wadsworth Publishing Company, 1990; 354 pages; ISBN 0 02871 971 9).
- *Principles of Voice Production*, Ingo R. Titze (Allyn & Bacon, 1994; 354 pages; ISBN 0 13717 893 X).
- *Secrets of Singing – Female Voice (Low & High Voice)*, Jeffrey Allen (Warner Bros, 2000; 378 pages; ISBN 0 76927 805 1).
- *Secrets of Singing – Male Voice (Low & High Voice)*, Jeffrey Allen (Warner Bros, 1999; 377 pages; ISBN 0 76927 804 3).
- *Singing – The Mechanism and the Technique*, William Vennard (Carl Fisher, 1967; 275 pages; ISBN 0 82580 055 2).
- *Singing & Imagination*: A Human Approach to a Great Musical Tradition, Thomas Hemsley (Oxford University Press, 1998; ISBN 0 19 879016 3).
- *Singing for the Stars – A Complete Program for Training Your Voice*, Seth Riggs (Alfred Publishing, 1992; ISBN 0 88284 528 4).
- *Structure of Singing – System and Art in Vocal Technique*, Richard Miller (Schirmer Books, 1996; 372 pages; ISBN 0 02 872660 X).
- *Teach Yourself Singing*, Susan Sutherland (McGraw Hill – NTC, 1996; 160 pages; ISBN 0 84423 902 X).

- *The Broadway Song Companion: An Annotated Guide to Music Theatre Literature* by Voice Type and Song Style, by David P. DeVenney (Scarecrow Press, 1998; ISBN 0 81083 373 5).
- *The Contemporary Singer – Elements of Vocal Technique*, Anne Peckham (Hal Leonard, 2000; 250 pages; ISBN 0 63400 797 1).
- *The New Voice Pedagogy*, Marilee David (The Scarecrow Press, Inc, Lanham, MD & London 1995; ISBN 0 8108 2943 6).
- *The Professional Singer's Handbook*, Gloria Rusch (Hal Leonard, 1998; 212 pages; ISBN 0 79358 851 0).
- *The Professional Vocalist – A Handbook for Commercial Singers and Teachers*, Rachel L. Lebon (Scarecrow Press, 1999; 146 pages; ISBN 0 8108 3565 7 / 0 8108 3566 5).
- *The Science of the Singing Voice*, J. Sundberg (Northern Illinois University Press, 1989; 226 pages; ISBN 0 87580 542 6).
- *The Third Line: The Opera Performer as Interpreter*, Daniel Helfgot with William O. Beeman (Schirmer Books, 1993; ISBN 0 02 871036 3).
- *Unlocking Your Voice: Freedom to Sing*, Esther Salaman (Kahn & Averill, 1999; ISBN 1 871082 70 6).
- *Vocal Authority: Singing Style and Ideology*, John Potter (Cambridge University Press, 1998; ISBN 0 521 56356 9).
- *Voice Tradition and Technology; A State-of-the-Art Studio*, Garyth Nair, Ron Nair (Singular Publishing group, 1999; 326 pages; ISBN 0 76930 028 6).
- *You Can Sing*, Jerald B. Stone (Music Sales Corp., 2002; 80 pages; ISBN 0 82561 515 1).

Internet

The Internet offers a wealth of information for singers. Some examples of informative websites:

- www.singers.com – Primarily A Cappella
- www.jazzsingers.com

- www.choralnet.com – Choral Net
- www.vocalist.org.uk – Vocalist
- www.scaredofthat.com – The Diction Domain
- www.van.org – Vocal Area Network (vocal ensemble music)
- www.voice-center.com (describes disorders of the voice and the larynx)
- www.voicefoundation.org – The Voice Foundation (research and study of the human

Looking for a teacher?

Some of the sites above have links to teachers. You can also locate a teacher through one of the following sites:

- www.nats.org – National Association of Teachers of Singing
- www.voiceteachers.com – Internet directory of teachers of singing
- www.musicstaff.com
- If you search for 'vocal teacher(s),' 'teacher(s) of singing', or 'voice teacher(s),' you'll probably find other sites as well. You can also look for online teaching: Search for 'vocal lessons online' or 'voice lessons online,' for example.

Lyrics

Looking for lyrics of a pop song, a jazz standard, or an aria? The Internet can help you. Visit one of the following sites, or use a search engine to search for the word 'lyrics,' combined with the name of the song or the name of the artist.

- www.aria-database.com (arias only)
- www.lyricsfind.com
- www.lyricsfreak.com
- www.lyricsheaven.net
- www.lyricsprovider.com
- www.top100lyrics.com
- www.lyricalline.com (site for songwriters)

Choirs

Looking for a choir to join? If you search 'choirs' or 'choir links' you'll find various pages that can link you to choirs at different levels and in numerous styles.

Associations and societies

Numerous singers' associations and societies can be found on the Internet too. Some examples:

- American Choral Directors Association (ACDA), www.acdaonline.org
- Association of British Choral Directors (ABCD), www.abcd.org.uk
- Australian Association of Men Barbershop Singers (AAMBS), www.aambs.org.au
- Barber Shop Singers Society for the Preservation and Encouragement of Barber Shop Quartet Singing in America, www.spebsqsa.org
- British Association of Barbershop Singers (BABS), www.singbarbershop.com
- British Voice Association, www.british-voice-association.com
- Chorus America, www.chorusamerica.org
- Contemporary A Cappella Association (CASA), www.casa.org
- Ladies Association of British Barbershop Singers (LABBS), www.labbs.org.uk
- National Association of Choirs, www. ukchoirsassoc.co.uk
- Professional Women Singers Association (PWSA), pwsa.homestead.com
- Traditional Music and Song Association of Scotland, www.tmsa.info

CDs

If you want to broaden your scope on singing, consider listening to the following albums, each containing a wide variety of examples of vocal music.

- *Global Voices – Traditional, Sacred, Contemporary, various artists* (Music of the World, NC, 1998; MOW 146, MOW 147, MOW 148; box set, 3 CDs)
- *Voices! Voices! The Mighty Call – Choirs of the World*, presented by Joachim-Ernst Berend (Jaro Medien, Germany, 1998; JARO 421718/19; box set, 3 CDs; www.jaro.de

INDEX

Please check out the glossary on pages 205-211 for additional definitions of the terms used in this book.

THE TIPBOOK SERIES

Did you like this Tipbook? There are also Tipbooks for your fellow band or orchestra members! The Tipbook Series features various books on musical instruments, including the singing voice, in addition to Tipbook Music on Paper, Tipbook Amplifiers and Effects, *and* Tipbook Music for Kids and Teens - a Guide for Parents.

Every Tipbook is a highly accessible and easy-to-read compilation of the knowledge and expertise of numerous musicians, teachers, technicians, and other experts, written for musicians of all ages, at all levels, and in any style of music. Please check www.tipbook.com for up to date information on the Tipbook Series!

All Tipbooks come with Tipcodes that offer additional information, sound files and short movies at www.tipbook.com

Instrument Tipbooks

All instrument Tipbooks offer a wealth of highly accessible, yet well-founded information on one or more closely related instruments. The first chapters of each Tipbook explain the very basics of the instrument(s), explaining all the parts and what they do, describing what's involved in learning to play, and indicating typical instrument prices. The core chapters, addressing advanced players as well, turn you into an instant expert on the instrument. This knowledge allows you to make an informed purchase and get the most out of your instrument. Comprehensive chapters on maintenance, intonation, and tuning are also included, as well a brief section on the history, the family, and the production of the instrument.

Tipbook Acoustic Guitar

Tipbook Acoustic Guitar explains all of the elements that allow you to recognize and judge a guitar's timbre, performance, and playability, focusing on both steel-string and nylon-string instruments. There are chapters covering the various types of strings and their characteristics, and there's plenty of helpful information on changing and cleaning strings, on tuning and maintenance, and even on the care of your fingernails.

Tipbook Amplifiers and Effects – $14.95

Whether you need a guitar amp, a sound system, a multi-effects unit for a bass guitar, or a keyboard amplifier, *Tipbook Amplifiers and Effects* helps you to make a good choice. Two chapters explain general features (controls, equalizers, speakers, MIDI, etc.) and figures (watts, ohms, impedance, etc.), and further chapters cover the specifics of guitar amps, bass amps, keyboard amps, acoustic amps, and sound systems. Effects and effect units are dealt with in detail, and there are also chapters on microphones and pickups, and cables and wireless systems.

Tipbook Cello – $14.95

Cellists can find everything they need to know about their instrument in *Tipbook Cello.* The book gives you tips on how to select an instrument and choose a bow, tells you all about the various types of strings and rosins, and gives you helpful tips on the maintenance and tuning of your instrument. Basic information on electric cellos is included as well!

Tipbook Clarinet – $14.95

Tipbook Clarinet sheds light on every element of this fascinating instrument. The knowledge presented in this guide makes trying out and selecting a clarinet much easier, and it turns you into an instant expert on offset and in-line trill keys, rounded or French-style keys, and all other aspects of the instrument. Special chapters are devoted to reeds (selecting, testing, and adjusting reeds), mouthpieces and ligatures, and maintenance.

Tipbook Electric Guitar and Bass Guitar – $14.95

Electric guitars and bass guitars come in many shapes and sizes. *Tipbook Electric Guitar and Bass Guitar* explains all of their features and characteristics, from neck profiles, frets, and types of wood to different types of pickups, tuning machines, and — of course — strings. Tuning and advanced do-it-yourself intonation techniques are included.

Tipbook Drums – $14.95

A drum is a drum is a drum? Not true — and *Tipbook Drums* tells you all the ins and outs of their differences, from the type of wood to the dimensions of the shell, the shape of the bearing edge, and the drum's hardware. Special chapters discuss selecting drum sticks, drum heads, and cymbals. Tuning and muffling, two techniques a drummer must master to make the instrument sound as good as it can, are covered in detail, providing step-by-step instructions.

Tipbook Flute and Piccolo – $14.95

Flute prices range from a few hundred to fifty thousand dollars and more. *Tipbook Flute and Piccolo* tells you how workmanship, materials, and other elements make for different instruments with vastly different prices, and teaches you how to find the instrument that best suits your or your child's needs. Open-hole or closed-hole keys, a B-foot or a C-foot, split-E or donut, inline or offset G? You'll be able to answer all these questions — and more — after reading this guide.

Tipbook Keyboard and Digital Piano – $14.95

Buying a home keyboard or a digital piano may find you confronted with numerous unfamiliar terms. *Tipbook Keyboard and Digital Piano* explains all of them in a very easy-to-read fashion — from hammer action and non-weighted keys to MIDI, layers and splits, arpeggiators and sequencers, expression pedals and multi-switches, and more, including special chapters on how to judge the instrument's sound, accompaniment systems, and the various types of connections these instruments offer.

Tipbook Music for Kids and Teens – a Guide for Parents – $14.95

How do you inspire children to play music? How do you inspire them to practice? What can you do to help them select an instrument, to reduce stage fright, or to practice effectively? What can you do to make practice fun? How do you reduce sound levels and

prevent hearing damage? These and many more questions are dealt with in *Tipbook Music for Kids and Teens – a Guide for Parents and Caregivers.* The book addresses all subjects related to the musical education of children from pre-birth to pre-adulthood.

Tipbook Music on Paper – $14.95

Tipbook Music on Paper – Basic Theory offers everything you need to read and understand the language of music. The book presumes no prior understanding of theory and begins with the basics, explaining standard notation, but moves on to advanced topics such as odd time signatures and transposing music in a fashion that makes things really easy to understand.

Tipbook Piano – $14.95

Choosing a piano becomes a lot easier with the knowledge provided in *Tipbook Piano*, which makes for a better understanding of this complex, expensive instrument without going into too much detail. How to judge and compare piano keyboards and pedals, the influence of the instrument's dimensions, different types of cabinets, how to judge an instrument's timbre, the difference between laminated and solid wood soundboards, accessories, hybrid and digital pianos, and why tuning and regulation are so important: Everything is covered in this handy guide.

Tipbook Saxophone – $14.95

At first glance, all alto saxophones look alike. And all tenor saxophones do too — yet they all play and sound different from each other. *Tipbook Saxophone* discusses the instrument in detail, explaining the key system and the use of additional keys, the different types of pads, corks, and springs, mouthpieces and how they influence timbre and playability, reeds (and how to select and adjust them) and much more. Fingering charts are also included!

Interactive Books with TIPCODES

Tipbook Trumpet and Trombone, Flugelhorn and Cornet – $14.95

The Tipbook on brass instruments focuses on the smaller horns listed in the title. It explains all of the jargon you come across when you're out to buy or rent an instrument, from bell material to the shape of the bore, the leadpipe, valves and valve slides, and all other elements of the horn. Mouthpieces, a crucial choice for the sound and playability of all brasswinds, are covered in a separate chapter.

Tipbook Violin and Viola – $14.95

Tipbook Violin and Viola covers a wide range of subjects, ranging from an explanation of different types of tuning pegs, fine tuners, and tailpieces, to how body dimensions and the bridge may influence the instrument's timbre. Tips on trying out instruments and bows are included. Special chapters are devoted to the characteristics of different types of strings, bows, and rosins, allowing you to get the most out of your instrument.

Tipbook Vocals - The Singing Voice – $14.95

Tipbook Vocals –The Singing Voice helps you realize the full potential of your singing voice. The book, written in close collaboration with classical and non-classical singers and teachers, allows you to discover the world's most personal and precious instrument without reminding you of anatomy class. Topics include breathing and breath support, singing loudly without hurting your voice, singing in tune, the timbre of your voice, articulation, registers and ranges, memorizing lyrics, and more. The main purpose of the chapter on voice care is to prevent problems.

International editions

The Tipbook Series is also available in Spanish, French, German, Dutch, Italian, Swedish, and Chinese. For more information, please visit us at www.tipbook.com.

TIPBOOK SERIES MUSIC AND MUSICAL INSTRUMENTS

Tipbook Acoustic Guitar
ISBN 978-1-4234-6523-2, HL00332802 – $14.95

Tipbook Amplifiers and Effects
ISBN 978-1-4234-6277-4, HL00332776 – $14.95

Tipbook Cello
ISBN 978-1-4234-5623-0, HL00331904 – $14.95

Tipbook Clarinet
ISBN 978-1-4234-6524-9, HL00332803 – $14.95

Tipbook Drums
ISBN 978-90-8767-102-0, HL00331474 – $14.95

Tipbook Electric Guitar and Bass Guitar
ISBN 978-1-4234-4274-5, HL00332372 – $14.95

Tipbook Flute & Piccolo
ISBN 978-1-4234-6525-6, HL00332804 – $14.95

Tipbook Home Keyboard and Digital Piano
ISBN 978-1-4234-4277-6, HL00332375 – $14.95

Tipbook Music for Kids and Teens
ISBN 978-1-4234-6526-3, HL00332805 – $14.95

Tipbook Music on Paper – Basic Theory
ISBN 978-1-4234-6529-4, HL00332807 – $14.95

Tipbook Piano
ISBN 978-1-4234-6278-1, HL00332777 – $14.95

Tipbook Saxophone
ISBN 978-90-8767-101-3, HL00331475 – $14.95

Tipbook Trumpet and Trombone, Flugelhorn and Cornet
ISBN 978-1-4234-6527-0, HL00332806 – $14.95

Tipbook Violin and Viola
ISBN 978-1-4234-4276-9, HL00332374 – $14.95

Tipbook Vocals – The Singing Voice
ISBN 978-1-4234-5622-3, HL00331949 – $14.95

Check www.tipbook.com for additional information!